WHY HISTORY MATTERS

JOHN TOSH

First published 2008 by
PALGRAVE MACMILLAN
Houndmills, Basingstoke, Hampshire RG21 6XS and
175 Fifth Avenue, New York, N.Y. 10010
Companies and representatives throughout the world

PALGRAVE MACMILLAN is the global academic imprint of the Palgrave Macmillan division of St. Martin's Press, LLC and of Palgrave Macmillan Ltd. Macmillan® is a registered trademark in the United States, United Kingdom and other countries. Palgrave is a registered trademark in the European Union and other countries.

ISBN-13: 9–780–230–52148–3   paperback
ISBN-10: 0–230–52148–7   paperback

This book is printed on paper suitable for recycling and made from fully managed and sustained forest sources. Logging, pulping and manufacturing processes are expected to conform to the environmental regulations of the country of origin.

A catalogue record for this book is available from the British Library.

A catalog record for this book is available from the Library of Congress.

Library of Congress Catalog Card Number: 2008020592

10   9   8   7   6   5   4   3
17   16   15   14   13   12   11   10   09

Printed and bound in China

For Caroline

Contents

Preface

Judging by the tenor of political debate and the coverage of the media, most people in Britain think that in a fast-moving world history has little or nothing to offer to a rational public discourse. Time and again, complex policy issues are placed before the public without adequate explanation of how they have come to assume their present shape, and without any hint of the possibilities that are disclosed by the record of the past. Historians – who should be doing most to correct this view – hold back from an overzealous concern to uphold their scholarly integrity. Yet this is a critical dimension of citizenship. To know that the past can illuminate the contours of the present is to be better equipped to make intelligent decisions about difficult public issues. Within Whitehall there is some acknowledgement of that proposition, and its practical consequences have been analysed in a number of studies of the influence of history and historians on policy-making at the highest level. The machinery of government is not my concern. My purpose in this book is to show how a more widespread understanding of historical thinking might bring closer the ideal of the critical citizen.

Making progress in this project requires a re-ordering of priorities on the part of the schools, the media and historians themselves. Such a programme has been advocated many times in the past. But the present is a particularly auspicious moment for two reasons. First, history is enjoying unprecedented exposure in the public media. It is more securely established in common culture than at any time in the past century, and while the main focus is on entertainment, it nevertheless provides a starting point for a critical engagement between past and present. Secondly, enough historians are now exploring ways of bringing their knowledge to bear on topical issues – through broadcasting and the Internet, as well as in print – to demonstrate that history potentially has a major public role.

Why History Matters does not put forward a comprehensive rationale for the study of history. I do not explore arguments of an aesthetic, symbolic or spiritual kind. My concern is a practical one: to make the case that history is a critical resource for the active citizen in a representative democracy. I do not believe that this is the only reason for valuing history: if I did, the case for studying medieval and early modern history would be distinctly muted. But the arguments in favour of the practical approach are not often heard, partly because historians tip-toe round the issue of 'relevance', and partly because the practical yield of academic history is often confused with explicitly political renderings of the past. In fact, history offers two different forms of empowerment. On the one hand, it can be used to intensify the sense of belonging to a group (be it nation or community) by anchoring it securely in shared narratives of the past. On the other hand, it can empower through enhancing the intellectual resources available to the active citizen. In practice this distinction is far from clear-cut, since there is much trading across the boundary. But it nevertheless expresses a significant demarcation: the first tends towards rhetorical confirmation, while the second is about intellectual empowerment. This book explores and evaluates the second function. It identifies the basic features of historical thinking – or historical mindedness – and shows how they can be applied to contemporary concerns.

This line of argument has important implications for education in citizenship, which has been an objective of government policy since 1997. History has an acknowledged place in the citizenship curriculum, but it is primarily viewed as an adjunct to national identity and the politics of multiculturalism, with the risk that students will be passive consumers of pre-determined identities. My contention is that the real value of history lies in equipping young people with a distinctive mode of thinking which can be critically applied to the present. Without such a perspective they will have a greatly impoverished sense of the possibilities inherent in the present; they will be unlikely to be able to distinguish between what is ephemeral and what is enduring in present circumstances; and the ongoing processes of change unfolding in our own time will be closed to them. These are the essentials of 'thinking with history', and the following chapters demonstrate their place in the mental equipment of the active, participating citizen.

Two contested concepts have a bearing on the content of this book: *applied history* and *public history*. The first has an equivocal track record, having often been identified with politically driven research or with overly schematic research agendas. However, it is central to the argument of this book that historical knowledge can be usefully 'applied' in ways that are defined by neither politics nor ideology. 'Applied history' refers here to historical knowledge that has been built up in pursuit of academic ends but which *also* has a bearing on current public concerns. 'Public history' needs careful definition because the term has come to mean so many different things. The common factor is that history is the property of 'the public' rather than academia, in the sense that the laity are the principal audience. Most discussions of public history locate it in heritage sites, museums or the media. In this book I take 'public history' to mean also the work of dissemination that academic historians undertake to place their knowledge at the disposal of the public. This is only one dimension of public history – often omitted from standard definitions – but it is indispensable for the realisation of a socially responsible applied history.

This is not a work of theory, but an aid to practical thinking. Instead of arguing from first principles, it seeks to demonstrate the practical relevance of history. The illustrative examples – some of them quite extended – are therefore central to the argument. They have been chosen primarily with a British readership in mind, but that does not mean that they are confined to the UK. I have also drawn on overseas material that is likely to be familiar to British readers – primarily in the USA and the Middle East. The text itself follows a straightforward structure. The Prologue establishes the public importance of a critical history in relation to one of the most contentious issues of recent years: the invasion of Iraq. Chapter 1 places academic history in the context of heritage and identity history – viewed by some as competitors, by others as partners. The next three chapters distil the essential components of historical thinking and their application to the present day: Chapter 2 pursues the implications of the gulf between past and present; Chapter 3 analyses the role of process and trajectory in illuminating the present; and Chapter 4 evaluates the insights and distortions which stem from the use of historical analogy. Chapter 5 offers an extended case-study on the history of the family in Britain, demonstrating both the political manipulation of the past and the constructive part that historians can play in placing a fundamental aspect of our lives in perspective. Chapters 6 and 7 consider the question of audience, first from the perspective of the historical profession, then in the context of citizenship.

* * * * * * *

This is a short book, but it would have taken much longer to write without a sabbatical leave from Roehampton University and a Research Leave Award from the Arts and Humanities Research Council: I am grateful to both of them.

In ranging so widely I have incurred many debts to friends and colleagues; my thanks to Gill Bennett, David Cannadine, Penelope Corfield, Simon Ditchfield, Vivien Hart, Jennifer Hicks, Boyd Hilton, Jorma Kalela, Peter Lee, Howell Lloyd, Michael Mason, Paul McGilchrist, Avner Offer, Mike Pinnock, Michael Roper, Jean Seaton, Martin Sheppard, John Simpson, Alastair Smith, Daniel Snowman and Simon Szreter. In 2006 I was fortunate enough to spend two months in Australia, where the debate about public history is a good deal further advanced than in the UK. Arthur Busch, Paula Hamilton, Sylvia Lawson and Klaus Neumann did much to enlighten me about that debate. The book is dedicated, with love, to Caroline White who has been a meticulous and perceptive reader of every chapter, and who needs no convincing that history is a profoundly practical subject.

John Tosh
London

Prologue: Britain in Iraq

As British troops entered Basra in April 2003, few people in Britain realised that this was not the first time. Nearly ninety years earlier, in November 1914, a force of 5000 men had captured the city, at a cost of 489 casualties.[1] The circumstances were very different, of course. The world in which that occupation took place has virtually disappeared. In 2003 Britain acted as a junior partner of the US in the full glare of world publicity; in 1914 Britain acted alone, and the occupation of Basra was an obscure sideshow in a much wider conflict. The Raj in India was still at the heart of Britain's global interests, and Iraq mattered because of its place in communications with India. For that reason the campaign was organised from Bombay using mostly Indian troops. The adversary in Basra was not 'Iraqi' or Arab, but the forces of the Ottoman Empire. In fact, Iraq did not yet exist. The British name for it – Mesopotamia – was also a fiction: the country was administered by the Turks as three free-standing provinces, of which Basra was one. So the occupation of 1914 hardly prefigured that of 2003. But the aftermath of 1914 *is* highly relevant to understanding the situation faced by the Anglo-American coalition from 2003 onwards. Basra was placed under military administration, while British forces gradually advanced northwards, taking Baghdad in 1917. At the end of the war, Britain was the obvious choice to take over the country from the defeated Turks. But instead of exercising complete sovereignty Britain administered Iraq as a Mandate of the League of Nations, and was in theory accountable to the new body. The Mandate continued until 1934, after which Britain withdrew to a position of informal influence, which ended only with the overthrow of the Iraqi monarchy in 1958.

That period provides food for thought in two ways. First, it directs attention to the intentions of the occupiers. During the 1920s British rule in Iraq was presented as an experiment in democratic state-building; when self-interest was acknowledged, it focused on the security of communications with India (at a time when the air route from Britain was being developed). What was left unstated was the rapidly growing significance of Iraq as an oil producer. By the First World War oil was the preferred fuel for the Royal Navy, and it was in short supply. At the time when Britain took over in Iraq, no oil had actually been found, but it was known to exist in large quantities in the north of the country. Well before drilling began around Kirkuk in 1927, oil was central to British interests in Iraq. As Marian Kent has put it, 'by 1920 Mesopotamian oil, still commercially as hypothetical as ever, had come to occupy a major place in British diplomatic and military concerns in the Middle East'.[2] Little of that concern was reflected in public statements about the Mandate.

The second point concerns Iraqi resistance. The British relied primarily on the minority Sunni community to staff the administration. The Shiites were accordingly the backbone of the resistance, though the participation of Sunnis and Kurds belies the notion that this was no more than a sectarian conflict. The rebellion of 1920 cost about 6000 Arab and 500 British and Indian lives: it was sufficiently serious to prompt the British to abandon direct rule, and instead to govern through a client regime. But the appointment of King Faisal (also a Sunni) in 1921 did not fundamentally alter the situation, since he was widely viewed as a British stooge. Major revolts occurred in 1923 and 1931, involving both Arabs and Kurds. The difference was that now the British relied less on ground troops, and more on aerial bombing. The RAF became a regular arm of the administration, especially to extract taxes from recalcitrant communities. After a visit to the country in 1925, the Colonial Secretary commented, 'If the writ of King Faisal runs effectively through his kingdom, it is entirely due to British aeroplanes. . . . If the aeroplanes were removed tomorrow, the whole structure would inevitably fall to pieces'.[3]

Calling to mind this history now is open to the objection that it consigns Iraq to a repetitive cycle from which there can be no escape because it is pre-ordained. That view can only be sustained if the impact of present-day contingencies is set aside. The point of these precedents is rather to broaden awareness of the possible – or likely – outcomes of external intervention in Iraq today. The occupation may or may not be driven by the politics of oil, but knowing something of the Mandate era might induce a healthy scepticism about official statements to the contrary. Of specific relevance to the British would be an enquiry into how their reception by the population of Basra today may be conditioned by their previous experience of conquest and colonial administration. Most critical of all, the naive expectations about the stability of post-Saddam Iraq might have been tempered by some awareness of the record of the Mandate. The difficulties of Faisal's regime in establishing its authority while visibly relying on the military support of an occupying power should have suggested, at the very least, a cautious estimation of the prospects for stable and secure administration once the war was over.

This interpretation of the British Mandate in Iraq can be found in a number of histories published since the 1970s – notably in the work of Peter Sluglett.[4] But none of it was in the public domain in Britain during the run-up to war in 2002–3. The mounting sense of crisis produced an immense volume of press comment. Almost all of it either expanded on the horrors perpetrated by Saddam, or speculated about the motives of the Bush administration. For most analysts, the relevant time-depth extended no further back than the first Gulf War in 1991. The major exception was the repeated reference to the era of appeasement in the 1930s: Saddam was widely compared to Adolf Hitler, as an aggressive dictator whose ambitions must be nipped in the bud before his arsenal grew any bigger. Conversely, several commentators who advocated restraint relied on the lesson of Eden's impetuous attack on Nasser during the Suez crisis of 1956. These were rhetorical, moralising responses, which rode roughshod over yawning differences of context, and they further distracted the public from the perspectives that could be learned from the earlier history of Iraq itself.[5]

The almost exclusive focus of the press in 2003 on these imagined 'parallels' is telling evidence of the impoverishment of historical awareness in our society. Faced with the prospect of war in a foreign country about which they knew little, the British public should have been equipped with the relevant historical material, presented with due respect for the limits of applied history. Some blame must be attached to the editorial priorities of press and television. But the problem goes deeper. History education in its broadest sense is in a state of crisis. History teaching in schools is designed to accommodate as many different demands on content as possible, at the expense of conveying what historical perspective means, and how it might usefully be applied to current issues. At the same time, professional historians are strangely reluctant to adopt the role of expert. If they reach out to the public, it is usually to popularise academic history of a conventional kind; and most historians do not do even that, preferring to address only their academic peers. The consequence is a significant democratic deficit. Active participation in our political culture depends on many attributes, but critical knowledge is consistently downplayed in current debates about citizenship. This book explains how historical reasoning can be applied to the present, why the expertise of historians is needed in the public sphere, and why our democracy would be the stronger for it.

1

Contending Histories

There has never been a time...when, except in the most general sense, a study of history provides so little instruction for our present day.'[1] That statement was made by Tony Blair in 2003 in a speech to the United States Congress. The immediate context was the invasion of Iraq – just completed – and the political need to refute the dire lessons that could be drawn from the history of that country. The speech was widely taken to express the Prime Minister's indifference towards history. But it also reflected a much more widespread scepticism about the practical benefits of historical perspective. Belief in history's capacity to understand the present and enlarge its sense of possibilities has never been weaker. The foundations for such a history are poorly laid in school education. The news media draw on historical material only fitfully, and on many key topics not at all. For the most part the electorate is not in a position to apply historical perspective to the evaluation of current policies and attitudes. The British public, it has been said, suffers from Historical Attention Span Deficit Disorder.[2]

It may seem perverse to begin a book about the public role of history with a lament for its marginal status in Britain today. For has not history become a staple of the TV channels, and is not an increasing proportion of people's leisure time taken up by family history, visits to historic sites, and more variants of collecting than have yet been documented? Should not historians be grateful that their subject has become 'the new gardening'? The problem is that – with the exception of a few TV programmes – none of these activities brings historical perspective to bear on issues of topical importance. Indeed, their very popularity diminishes the public space that is available for that kind of analysis. We are confronted by the paradox of a society which is immersed in the past yet detached from its history.

Thinking with history: a citizen's resource

Debate about the role of history in our culture turns on two very different issues. The first concerns the political ends that history might serve, variously conceived as national heritage, group identity and political ideology. The question raised by such histories is not whether they are valid *as history*, but what kind of social role they perform, and this has become a significant battleground of cultural politics. The second issue concerns the validity of history as a branch of knowledge, in the light of the Postmodernist assault on its credentials: can 'history' deliver sound knowledge of the past, or is it better understood as a projection – or a kaleidoscope – of very contemporary cultural preoccupations? The latter position may characterise only a small proportion of academics – most of them not historians – but there is considerable cultural support for a lazy relativism which sees one perspective on the past as being as good as another. What neither cultural politics nor Postmodernism does is to evaluate the kinds of practical understanding which can be derived from history: the first because it values outcome over process, the second because it refutes the notion of applicability altogether. So it is hardly surprising that there is a very low level of public awareness of how history might offer insights into the contemporary world.

Yet there is no mystery about those forms of practical reasoning. Nor do they subvert the accepted principles of scholarship. They are implicit in the nature of historical enquiry itself. A public role for history does not mean imposing a practical agenda on all research; what it foregrounds is the need to be alert to the implications that many of its findings have for public understanding. Following the American cultural historian Carl Schorske, we might call this 'thinking with history'. Whereas thinking *about* history is a general form of meaning-making without practical import, thinking *with* history is the activity which enables us to 'orient ourselves in the living present'. In Schorske's account, thinking with history has two modes. On the one hand, it produces images of the past, against which we position ourselves by difference or resemblance. On the other hand, it discloses the temporal flows which generate narratives of change, out of which our historical present is formed.[3] Identifying what is distinctive about the present, enlarging our awareness of the possibilities inherent in the present, and situating the present in the processes which link it with the past and the future – each of these is consistent with the accepted norms of historical scholarship. They are what it might mean to 'think with history'.

The least contentious application of historical reasoning lies in the recognition of the past as an almost limitless experiential resource. The range of activity, mentality and reflection uncovered from past societies goes far beyond what could be imagined using only the resources of the contemporary world. This record of human creativity is an important part of our armoury for facing the future. It seldom affords a basis for prediction, but it feeds the imagination about the potential for alternatives in the future. It is also a powerful antidote to any notion of a predestined path.[4] Reconstructing the different world of the past also has more specific applications. Long forgotten traditions of thought may acquire fresh salience in the light of changes which are occurring now. Sometimes research yields an antecedent which is strikingly at variance with what is lazily assumed to be immutable or 'natural' today; the right conditions are thus created for evaluating the possibility of change in the future. Comparing our own society with one at an earlier stage of development throws into relief what is distinctive and what is commonplace or recurrent about our social arrangements. Anthropologists have long fulfilled part of this brief. What historians supply is the time continuum, which demonstrates the extent of variation within our own culture. Reflecting on the history of childhood, Philippe Ariès pointed out how difficult it was to distinguish the characteristics of the living present 'except by means of the differences which separate them from the related but never identical aspects of the past'.[5]

The other essential ingredient of the historian's perspective is to explain the process of development and change which led from the different world of 'then' to the familiar world of 'now'. Our understanding of the world around us is inhibited by an excessive emphasis on day-to-day changes. This relentless presentism promotes superficial analysis. It obscures the deeper reality that all experience takes place in a temporal flow which exerts as much influence on our current condition as the synchronic and the contemporaneous. Hence the relevance of history to so many current concerns. The conflicts which beset the NHS today cannot be understood without taking account of the ideological climate in which it was founded and its cumulative erosion since then by financial and political calculation. International crises stand in no less need of historical perspective. The present situation in Iraq – as the Prologue showed – makes little sense without considering the full span of its twentieth-century history. On that depends an understanding of the dynamics of sectarian conflict and of anti-Western sentiment. Only a historical perspective can reveal the longer-term trajectories which structure so much of the world around us. Those trajectories have both negative and positive import. They can be invoked as reassurance for the future, but they may also facilitate a more realistic diagnosis of social ills. R. H. Tawney likened the society of his day to a structure standing on deep foundations: to grasp the meaning of the cracks and the stability of the edifice, he said, we must investigate the quality of those foundations.[6]

Tawney believed that his metaphor conveyed an important lesson in practical history that his contemporaries stood sorely in need of. The lack of historical awareness that he addressed seventy years ago is still prevalent today. Yet at any point up to 1914 it was axiomatic among educated people that the past could be read for insights into the present. Aspirant members of the political elite studied history as a storehouse of practical examples in the art of governing. New nations searched for their validating origins in the mists of time. Older nations anxiously surveyed earlier instances of decline in order to assess their own prospects. Liberalism and socialism were both grounded in a sense of the logic of history. In the generation before 1914 only a small avant-garde of philosophers and artists dissented from the authority of history. The First World War unravelled the consensus in this as in so many other areas. The lessons of the past and the logic of history that the statesmen had invoked in support of national objectives before the war were now discredited. The modernist movement in the visual arts and in literature searched for new forms untrammelled by the heritage of the past. In society at large, the pace of technological advance meant that modernity became completely identified with the new. In more recent decades that trend has been intensified by the onset of globalisation and the electronic revolution in communications. These developments are generally construed as 'progress', but progress without a hinterland in the past. The countervailing intimations of disaster held out first by nuclear weapons and now by global warming also encourage belief in a world which is fashioned anew, to all practical purposes without a history.

The same holding of history at arm's length is apparent in political discourse. For several decades after the Second World War, the worldwide conflict between the West and the Communist bloc placed a premium on shared historical narratives. The Cold War only made sense when regarded as the outcome of developments which had been unfolding since 1945, if not 1917. Yet by the time the Cold War ended in the early 1990s, the public grasp on recent history was already slackening. 'Most young men and women at the century's end', wrote Eric Hobsbawm in 1994, 'grow up in a sort of permanent present lacking any organic relation to the public past of the times they live in.'[7] The collapse of Communism means that there is now even less reason to hold on to a historical perspective that extends back beyond people's adult memories. Within Britain the content of politics is increasingly detached from any sense of the past. Both major parties have employed strongly modernising rhetoric – Labour under Harold Wilson and the Conservatives under Edward Heath. Margaret Thatcher's appeal to the Victorian past, though productive of considerable debate at the time, seems like an anomaly in retrospect. Having ceased to offer competing visions of society, the Tories and Labour now have little reason to invoke the past. Indeed, the world before 1997 is best ignored – by the Tories in order to distance themselves from Thatcher's legacy, and by New Labour in order to shake off any association with the self-destructive factionalism of the party during the 1980s. Politically the past has become 'an embarrassment, a burden to be escaped rather than a patrimony to be reclaimed'.[8] Today's political elite is less minded and less qualified to draw on the lessons of history than were any of its predecessors.

The charms of heritage

If political leaders in Britain today show a marked lack of historical sense, it does not follow that the state is indifferent to history.
The past twenty years have seen an unprecedented involvement by
official bodies in what has come to be called 'heritage'. The numer-
ous activities grouped under this label enjoy genuine popularity,
but since the establishment of the Department of Heritage in 1992
and the Heritage Lottery Fund in 1994 they have become a focus
of government policy, and they are increasingly dependent on state
funding. 'Heritage' itself defies precise analysis – 'a nomadic term
which travels easily' is how Raphael Samuel described it.[9] But its
'core business' – a phrase which accurately conveys the prevailing
commercial ethos – is the conservation, transmission and enjoyment
of visible survivals from the past. Heritage nurtures a relationship
between ordinary people and their historical environment. At one
level it denotes the local appreciation of any survival from the past,
be it a hedgerow or the exposed beams of a sixteenth-century inn. At
another level it refers to major cultural institutions: the centralised
and well funded efforts of English Heritage to maintain historic
buildings, or the underwriting of large capital projects by the Heritage Lottery Fund. Those two extremes capture the tension at the
heart of heritage between amateur enthusiasm on the one hand
and policy-driven initiatives on the other. Yet there is more common ground than might be supposed between the country house,
the steam preservation society and a local conservation group. The
visible remains of the past – often tidied up and sometimes recon-
structed – are intended to stimulate the imagination. The past, it
is claimed in countless brochures, can be experienced or re-enacted
(as in a Day in a Tudor Kitchen, or a journey on the foot-plate of a
steam locomotive). And since neither specialist expertise nor textbook knowledge is required, the experience is accessible to all. Hence
the claim that heritage is telling evidence of an expanding historical
culture, and thus a genuinely democratic phenomenon.

For more than twenty years, heritage has been the subject of angry
denunciation, directed first at the idolisation of the stately home,
and later at the role of the state in manufacturing a cultural consensus about the past. Left-wing critics like Robert Hewison and Patrick

Wright have emphasised the hidden political agenda which lies behind many manifestations of heritage.[10] It plays on a recoil from the less pleasant aspects of the present and encourages an escape into a more stable past, when society was governed by the 'traditional' values whose hold is so tenuous today: hence the appeal of paternalism represented by the traditional country house, or the skilled artisan celebrated at sites of the early Industrial Revolution. Heritage purveys a commodification of the past. Its dependence on material objects – whether genuine or manufactured in facsimile – further loads the dice in favour of a history populated by the wealthy and refined. When Prince Charles remarked 'our history is all around us', he was referring exclusively to buildings.[11] Many of our most popular heritage sites encourage a view of the past which is superficial, nostalgic and conformist; they are not so much a means of education as an adjunct to tourism.

The weakness of this critique is that it assumes a convergence of view between those who provide heritage and those who experience it. Visitors to stately homes or military museums do not necessarily buy into the ideology which informs the display. Consumers have their own interpretative standpoints, and they should not be subsumed in a condescending stereotype. This applies even more strongly to the world of make-your-own-heritage. As Raphael Samuel argued in *Theatres of Memory* (1994), historians should hesitate before dismissing occupations like family history and the collecting of old photographs. They attract some of the biggest numbers of any heritage activity, and they are largely independent of the cultural *dirigisme* of the major heritage institutions.

But from the perspective of this book, the weightiest charge against heritage concerns not its politics, but the damage it has done to historical consciousness. What heritage displaces is at least as important as the views it promotes. For large numbers of people heritage has become virtually synonymous with history. Yet the lens through which they are invited to view history is distorted because it tends to assimilate the past to the present. Apart from the beguiling differences of dress, people 'then' are taken to be fundamentally the same as us, which is why their way of life can be invoked to buttress the best of today's – or yesterday's – values. The past is treated as an extension of our own age. Part of the explanation for this lies in the solidly material basis of heritage. Because heritage deals primarily in the objects surviving from the past, it often fails to convey the extent of the gulf which divides us from our forebears – in mentality, culture and social values. The profound contrasts between 'us' and 'them', which can cast the present in really surprising light, are blurred. The same stress on conservation, display and experience places histori-cal explanation at a discount. The past is to be contemplated and admired, not analysed and interpreted. History then ceases to be an intellectual resource; its capacity to inform and unsettle the present is obscured by a screen of sentiment. David Lowenthal, one of the shrewdest commentators on heritage, points out: 'heritage . . . . is not an effort to know what actually happened but a profession of faith in a past tailored to present-day purposes'. Lowenthal regards heritage as valid and even admirable in its own terms, but in his view it should not be confused with history. In debates about cultural provision and educational policy, that distinction is all too often lost sight of.[12]

History as a culture of belonging

'Identity history' is a convenient label to refer to those representa-tions of the past which are organised around a group's stated need for a usable past: that is, a past which confirms and dignifies the group's identity and which focuses on little else. It falls into the same broad category as heritage, in that it answers a need to produce a past which supports a sense of group belonging in the present. But whereas 'heritage' most often refers to a top–down identity – typi-cally the nation – identity history works up from the grass roots. This is the terrain of the 'popular history-makers', as Roy Rosenzweig and David Thelen call them in their survey of American popular cultures of the past.[13] The logical starting point is the lines of descent, which endow the individual with a past beyond the limits of biological time. This is the basis of the current boom in family history: 7 per cent of all internet users in Britain have investigated their family history on line. As a cultural activity this is highly suggestive. Fam-ily research is obviously a response to the extremes of social and geographical mobility which have characterised the last century. Its appeal is increased by the contemporary sense of a crisis in family life, which endows the past with the attraction of stability.[14] Recent work has identified family history as a 'resurrective practice'; the bounds of mortality are enlarged by endowing ancestors with an afterlife in the minds of both the living and their descendants.[15]

Most family researchers will do no more than identify a handful of forebears. But for the more committed the goal is to place their forebears in a historically realised world – be it one of poverty or of respectability. Alex Haley's dramatic account of his slave ancestry in *Roots* (a 1970s bestseller in both printed and televised form) has been credited with a decisive role in popularising the idea that ordinary people might recover a fully realised past, and that a narrative of redemption could be constructed out of privation and abuse.[16] Yet, as a window on history, family research remains problematic because of its exclusive focus upon individuals. The TV series *Who Do You Think You Are?*, in which well known personalities are invited to track down their forebears, attracts large audiences, partly because so much is made of the social circumstances in which ancestors lived (in dire poverty, in some cases). But for most practitioners of family history the priority given to named individuals in the past works against a sense of social consciousness or social agency. Those who aspire to something more than a genealogy usually find that the sources simply do not permit a coherent account: the published family history is the prize exhibit of the genre, but it is achieved by a tiny number.

Family history may be one of the most popular leisure pursuits in Britain; but in political and social impact it is outstripped by history, which addresses the identity politics of communities rather than individuals. One of the liveliest features of the historical scene in Britain today is the diversity of identities which draw on history. Fifty years ago, only the nation had a history in the sense of an extended validating narrative (in the British case it was built around constitutional excellence at home and commercial enterprise overseas). History was believed to disclose the national character, and to provide the means of reinforcing its hold over the present. Today, the fact that national history no longer enjoys a popular monopoly has sharpened the arguments advanced in its defence, as was made very clear during the debates on the National Curriculum between 1990 and 1995. The television schedules are sufficient evidence that the genre of national history is far from dead. But the novelty of our times lies in the demand by other groups not only to feature in the national story, but to have their own distinct histories – women's history, black history, gay and lesbian history, and so on. Each of these is also the subject of important scholarly work, in which the cultural politics of identity is tempered by a sense of historical context. But at a popular level it is political morale which provides the driving force of identity history. History should tell us 'who we are'. The forebears who feature in such accounts suffered, endured, and resisted, occasionally making their mark against all the odds. Their role is to strengthen solidarity among the living, sustained by the heroism of their ancestors. Since history is integral to social visibility, reconstructing the past may also contribute to the recognition of one's own group by others. Indeed, one interpretation of multiculturalism is that it is as much about creating a conversation between cultures, as about protecting and promoting the heritage of any single group.

Over the past thirty years, identity history has helped to sustain a vibrant politics of diversity in Britain. The complacency of the approved forms of national history was ripe for challenge. No one who cares about a more equitable society can regret the part that history has played in increasing the pride and confidence of previously marginalised groups. But identity history has done little to foster a critical public history. Much of its content is a matter for affirmation rather than scholarly demonstration and debate. The form is linear, and the logic of the story may prevail over the need to place successive episodes in their historical context. The moral complexity of the past – and the present – is underplayed because so often a single emotional response is demanded. In situations of sectarian antagonism, promoting a one-dimensional past has especially negative consequences. The Irish-born philosopher Eamonn Callan recalls the stultifying effect of childhood lessons on the Easter Rising:

> if my pride in the blood sacrifice of 1916 hinges on disregard of
> the political potency of patience and compromise, I will hardly
> be sufficiently alert to their possible potency in the present.

What Callan calls a 'sentimental' approach to history elevates emotion over reason and induces a narrowed moral sensibility.[17]

Above all, identity history trades on a spurious identity between 'them' and 'us': 'we' are all signed up to the same struggle, all looking forward to its successful resolution. Ancestors are recruited to a contemporary agenda, whereas *their* identities would be much more faithfully captured by registering the yawning difference between their circumstances and ours. Twenty years ago Denise Riley created a stir among feminists by claiming that the category 'women' was 'a volatile collectivity', from which it followed that the apparent continuity of 'women's history' was an illusion; 'women' has always been understood relative to other categories which have also been subject to constant change.[18] Black history raises similar issues. The metaphor of 'roots', so prevalent in black studies since the publication of Alex Haley's book in 1976, carries the same essentialising import. White racism and an enduring African heritage are seen as permanent constituents of what it means to be black. Stuart Hall comments:

> Cultural identities come from somewhere, have histories. But, like everything which is historical, they undergo constant transformation. Far from being eternally fixed in some essentialised past, they are subject to the continuous 'play' of history, culture, power.[19]

Ethnic identity is in reality an indefinite process of movement and mediation, without fixity. Essentialising one's relation to people in the past robs them of their potential to bring today's assumptions and priorities into question.

If 'they' were in essential respects the same as 'us,' it follows that we can take credit for their achievements, and protest against their wrongs. One of the most powerful springs of present-day political identity is the collective memory of past injustices. History probably has more power over the living as a record of grievance, than of triumph. As well as strengthening group solidarity the injustices of the past may provide a focus for political action, in the shape of a demand for reparations. There was much reflection along these lines during the bicentenary of the British abolition of the slave trade in 1807. Campaigns for restitution certainly testify in a very direct way to the formidable power of history. But it is history of an attenuated

kind. The historical evidence of the slave trade is truly shocking, in
the sense that no one becoming acquainted with it for the first time
could be emotionally or morally untouched: it is a past with which
every generation must come to terms. But the story of the slave trade
contains its share of moral ambiguities; and neither its causes nor its
effects can be baldly stated. As for the meaning that the trade holds
for the present, retrospective indignation directed at wrongs deeply
woven into the fabric of history can divert attention from wrongs
which exist today and which may be remediable. Acknowledging
those complexities may not yield a quick political fix, but it enlarges
the topical relevance of the slave trade. One appropriate response
to the bicentenary is to pursue an analogy with human trafficking
today, registering what is enduring and what is distinctive to our
own time. Another is to consider the legacy of forced uprooting
among the black populations of Britain and the Americas today.

In many ways the narratives which sustain cultural identity in the
present are best considered not as history but as collective memory.
Like all forms of social recall, they are closely related to the requirements of the present, and they endure for as long as they have a
place in the consciousness of group members. Nor is this emphasis
on collective memory confined to the marginalised. It clearly operates in the sphere of national heritage also, where the royal palaces
and national rituals serve as recurrent reminders of a shared history, and where museums and the media maintain the memory of
exemplary wartime experiences.

Formal historical knowledge has traditionally been presented as
the antithesis of collective memory. That view has been forcefully
put by Pierre Nora, the great student of public memory in France.
'Memory is life', he says; history, on the other hand, is reconstruction; memory expresses group loyalty, whereas history 'belongs to
everyone and no one'. And it is characteristic of modern societies
that history supersedes memory. Nora speaks of the 'acceleration of
history'.[20] The sense that history is eliminating collective memory
is less obvious now than when Nora wrote in 1989, partly because
of the rapid growth of identity history. Indeed, in some countries – though not yet in Britain – the process appears to have been
reversed as historical understanding gives place to a culture of memory and commemoration.[21] At the same time, academic historians

take a closer interest in collective memory than an oil-and-water distinction might suggest. In the 1960s and 1970s the oral history movement began among professional and community historians, as a means of enriching the social record with evidence of ordinary lives beyond the scope of documentary sources. Today, collective memory is at the cutting edge of cultural history because of the insight it provides into the historical consciousness of ordinary people; shared memory comprises a repertoire of images of the past, adjusted over time to reflect changing circumstances and changing social values. In so far as identity history articulates a body of social memory, it reinforces certain community values, but as a record of information about the past it is rather less reliable. For a critical public history which aims to place the relationship between present and past in as objective a light as possible, the high profile of identity history is an uncertain asset.

The vicissitudes of 'relevant' history

Critics have for some time deplored the marginalisation of critical public history by heritage and identity history. As early as 1987, Robert Hewison warned of the dangers of history becoming absorbed into heritage.[22] Yet powerful rivals are not the only reason why critical public history has faltered in recent years. Historians themselves must bear some of the blame, on account of their enduring reluctance to turn their knowledge to public account. When history became professionalised in the mid-nineteenth century, it staked its credentials on its academic detachment and its privileged entrée into the remoteness of the past. The countervailing demands of nationalism meant that not all practitioners observed this austere code, but it remained the rallying cry of most historians.

Ever since the foundation of the discipline, voices have from time to time been raised against a narrowness of vision and an indifference to the wider public. In recent decades the weightiest of these voices was E. H. Carr in *What is History?* (1961). Carr defined history as 'an unending dialogue between past and present'; for him, the content of this dialogue consisted not of the minutiae of technical scholarship, but of the big questions of progress and development. One would have thought that Carr would have reflected a seismic shift in the historical profession. After all, during the twentieth century the most notable trend in historical scholarship was its intensifying relationship with the social sciences, which Carr fully endorsed. His book probably contributed to the turn by younger scholars towards new historical themes which spoke to topical concerns, like urban history and family history. But it was the subject-matter and methods of enquiry that were modified, not the relationship of historians to the public. Carr had little influence on the attitude of the historical profession as a whole. His book is still prescribed reading for undergraduates in British universities, but with the intention of provoking debate rather than demanding agreement. There was certainly nothing of Carr's dynamic yoking of past and present in the bleak picture of the historical profession given by David Cannadine in 1987. Academic history, he said, was 'an intellectual pastime for consenting adults in private':

> At the universities, as in the schools, the belief that history provides an education, that it helps us understand ourselves in time, or even that it explains something of how the present world came into being, has all but vanished.[23]

If these contributions to understanding the present were absent from university history teaching, they were even less likely to be pursued in any outreach programme. Twenty years on, very few university courses examine the role that historical expertise might play in contemporary society. When, in 1997, Richard J. Evans composed a defence of history modelled in part on Carr's book, he offered no social justification for historical enquiry, nor did he consider relations between historians and the wider public.[24]

Why, then, do most historians turn their backs on a social role which would increase their readership and contribute to public understanding? Partly the answer takes us back to the beginnings of the academic profession of history in the mid-nineteenth century. Leopold von Ranke and his colleagues were determined to establish a dignified role for the historian, independent of the political paymasters and patrons who had called the tune in the past. The new breed of research historian was to be dedicated to the study of the past on its own terms, employing to that end the most rigorous techniques of disinterested scholarship. This austere attitude to the past was called 'historicism': it soon became dominant in German universities, and in the late nineteenth century spread to Britain.[25] The aim of historical scholarship over the past 150 years has been to rescue the subject from the lay person's belief that it exists only in relation to the present. Explaining why the role of the modern scholar is so much less practical than it was in the early modern era, Keith Thomas emphasises the legacy of historicism: 'the empathetic understanding of alien cultures or forgotten modes of thought and expression' diverted scholars from the demands of relevance.[26] Ever since, the purists have insisted on an absolute distinction between the historical approach to the past and the practical approach to the past.[27] In 1920 the Manchester historian T. F. Tout defined the purist position in terms which resonate to this day. Historians must, he insisted, set their minds against 'a gross and direct utility'. The value of historical study was 'something broader, more indefinite, more impalpable'.[28]

Over time, this renunciation of relevance became almost a defining attribute of the historical profession, and it gave ample scope to highly individualistic scholars to treat their work as a personal quest. The social historian Richard Cobb claimed never to have given the social purpose of history a thought: 'the writing of history is one of the fullest and most rewarding expressions of an individual personality'.[29] A. J. P. Taylor also roundly rejected the idea that history could be useful, and this allowed him to communicate his brilliant but often perverse insights into twentieth-century history with a clear conscience; paradoxically his writings and broadcasts did more than anyone else's to inform popular opinion about the era of the two world wars. Writers such as these were products of a long tradition of social detachment, and their eminence in the profession perpetuated it.

But much more important are the very negative political associations that applied history acquired during the twentieth century. Today's historians have an even greater awareness of the dangers of 'relevance' than Ranke did. To the generation that lived through the Second World War, 'relevant history' had a very disturbing resonance indeed. The distortion of historical scholarship in Nazi

Germany and Stalinist Russia was widely known. Writing in the 1960s the Oxford Medievalist V. H. Galbraith put it bluntly:

> Recent experiments abroad have shown . . . that the study of history can be given a practical bias, but only at the cost of making it frankly propagandist . . . . You cannot, in fact, make history pay a dividend.[30]

Even today, according to Peter Mandler, historians shy away from considering the practical uses of their discipline 'for fear of stirring up dying chauvinist embers'.[31] It is not hard to think of political situations in the recent past which have evoked that kind of reservation. In Northern Ireland, as Keith Jeffrey has observed, the phrase 'applied history' had a chilling ring.[32] Personal experience of totalitarianism certainly helps to explain some of the academic hostility to 'relevance'. G. R. Elton was a refugee from Nazism and a champion of history 'for its own sake'. He blamed Carr for undermining this principle in *What is History?*, and made a vigorous counter-polemic in his own book *The Practice of History* (1967). Elton believed that Carr's views were a travesty which flowed from 'the cardinal error' of studying the past for the light it throws on the present.[33] A vocal minority of Marxists dissented, but Elton spoke for many of his profession. As recently as 1990, Roy Porter felt bound to insist that 'historians must not pen themselves up in ivory towers, spinning sophisticated philosophical denials of the continuities between past and present, and insisting that history teaches nothing (except that it teaches nothing)'.[34]

But Elton's sometimes intemperate diatribes against relevance in history already look dated. It is now less common to find 'history for its own sake' upheld with quite the same puritan zeal. Today's historians have a more sophisticated understanding of the interaction of past and present, and few regard the study of history 'for its own sake' as a sufficient rationale. Instead of totally rejecting 'relevance', historians more typically acknowledge the profound cultural value of their subject, while keeping at arm's length any notion of practical application. History has for long been justified as a stimulant to the imagination, since it is through the imagination that readers are able in part to enter lives and cultures very different from their own.[35] Theodore Zeldin says that historians are not soothsayers, but 'court jesters' whose 'detachment and humour' prevent us from taking ourselves too seriously.[36] These approaches align history firmly with the humanities as traditionally conceived: a cultural resource, not a guide to living. As Peter Mandler writes,

> the kinds of lessons history can teach are abstract, so abstract in fact, that we ought not to call them lessons at all; they lie among the kinds of human enrichment that we look to all the arts to provide.[37]

In similar vein, Ludmilla Jordanova defines history as 'an arena for contemplation', distancing it from any notion of application.[38]

This approach is valid in its own terms. Who could deny that history offers human enrichment? History certainly has the capacity to enhance our imaginative range and cultivate our empathy. And, as Zeldin asserts, it provides an ironic commentary on our doings. Such attitudes have yielded a rich harvest of great historical works from the Romantic era to the present day. The problem is that a respect for 'pure' historical research is so often taken to exclude serious engagement with a lay audience, on the grounds that the fount of scholarship will be polluted by extraneous considerations. In fact academic history and public history are less opposed than this stark contrast would suggest.

First, it is a mistake to suppose that practical forms of history will re-ignite the dying embers of chauvinism. 'Relevant' history does not necessarily dance to a nationalist tune. Most of the applied work cited later in this book aims to enhance public understanding of how our society is managed, and how it could be better managed – that is, politics in its broadest sense. In the field of nationalism, the contribution of a responsible public history is not to confirm group loyalties, but to subject them to a critical appraisal which distinguishes the conditions of their growth from the surrounding accretions of national myths. It is true that applied history is saddled with very negative associations, arising from the way it has been abused in the past and will doubtless be abused in the future. However, the responsible reaction is not to withdraw from the field, but to supply the public with accessible forms of history which are both scholarly and relevant.

Towards a critical applied history

In defending the integrity of applied history, the central argument of this book is that it can and should uphold the core principles of historical enquiry. The contrast drawn between 'pure' and 'applied' or 'practical' history is much overplayed. The choice of research topic may be influenced by a sensitivity to topical concerns, but the discipline of historical enquiry is resistant to taking a 'line.' As subsequent chapters will show, an effective applied history rests on the foundational concepts of historicism: the profound differences which distinguish the past from the present, and the processes over time which explain how the present has grown out of the past. One of the reasons why historians rarely proceed from a pre-determined policy agenda to a set of corresponding conclusions is that they are committed to a holistic approach, in which the object of enquiry is placed in its full social and cultural context. That explains why they are wary of confirming analogies with the past, especially those that rest on the selection of a single instance. This respect for context distinguishes them from economists and sociologists, who often draw on historical material, but in a highly structured way, designed to match a specific set of research questions. The contribution that historians can make to public debate is a by-product of broader enquiries based on the scholarly conventions of the discipline. That is why it makes sense to label it 'practical historicism'. A public role for history does not mean imposing a practical agenda on all research; what it foregrounds is the need to be alert to the implications that many of its findings have for civic discourse.

The public is sometimes represented as unduly vulnerable to specious interpretations of the past. But this overlooks the way in which historical findings reach the public. Scholarly expertise does not speak with one voice. Historians are cautious about laying claim to certainty or authority, even in the areas where they possess most expertise. They are habituated to an academic culture of challenge and dispute, in which knowledge is recognised to be provisional. The facts of the past may be beyond dispute, but they only 'count' because they are deemed to stand in a certain relationship with other facts – by cause or consequence, or by being subsumed in a larger category. These dispositions are matters of judgement on which professional disagreement is commonplace. Even greater uncertainty attaches to attempts to reconstruct the culture or mentality of a past society. Hence the idea that history teaches precise or prescriptive 'lessons' is untenable. Heritage, on the other hand, operates by different conventions. Its major tourist attractions are not sites of debate, but present uncontested one-dimensional perspectives on the past. Much of the value of critical public history lies in the sense of intellectual tension that it conveys. The more such history is communicated to a lay audience, the more it will become apparent that the merit of history lies in opening rather than in closing questions – in revealing options rather than insisting on answers.

* * * * * * *

It is clear from the other kinds of history circulating in Britain today that if academic historians do not meet the challenge of dissemination, no one else will, and we will be without a critical public history altogether. It may be objected that, in making this case, I have overplayed the distinction between academic history on the one hand, and heritage and identity history on the other. There is certainly considerable blurring at the margins. For example, heritage displays are often the product of scrupulous historical enquiry, while academics now give close attention to social memory. Scholarly works on black history also make their mark on works produced for the black community. But at the level of public consciousness the distinction between the popular and the professional is a real one. In the USA in the 1990s, Roy Rosenzweig and David Thelen conducted a survey of popular engagement with the past. They were anxious to demonstrate how much popular practice resembled that of the professional historian, and they were very critical of the dismissive attitude of some historians. But they were nevertheless clear about the distinctive contribution of the trained historian:

By providing context and comparison and offering structural explanations, history professionals can turn the differences between themselves and popular history-makers into assets rather than barriers.... They can help to counter false nostalgia about earlier eras. They can make people aware of possibilities for transforming the status quo.[39]

Heritage and identity history address a cultural and emotional desire to belong. Critical public history meets an aspiration to understand not just one's roots, but the issues on which all citizens are called upon to take a view.

2

Other Worlds

The year 1649 was an extraordinary moment in the history of England. Charles I was executed, a republic was declared, and the Army tightened its grip on the country. In this atmosphere of revolutionary ferment radical sects proliferated, their programmes ranging from pacifism to agrarian community-living. These maverick groups found no place in Cromwell's Commonwealth, and after the Restoration they slipped into obscurity. For a brief period in 1649–50 the Ranters attracted attention as the most radical and subversive group. They were itinerants drawn from the urban poor. They proclaimed what amounted to class war against the rich. They advocated free love without the trammels of marriage, and some of them practised it. But the Ranters were not forerunners of the secular hedonism of the twentieth century. First and foremost they were a religious sect, led by preachers. The rich were doomed because God would come soon 'to level the hills with the valleys, to lay the mountains low'; free love was consistent with the Ranters' belief that God was present in all material things and all human beings. The opportunity for new ways of living in the social turmoil of the 1640s was proclaimed in language which upheld the central importance of faith.[1]

The world of the Ranters is remote from us in time and atmosphere. It might be dismissed as an antiquarian curiosity. Indeed, for a long time it was known only to a handful of specialists. What propelled the Ranters and other radical groups into public consciousness was the publication in 1972 of Christopher Hill's *The World Turned Upside Down*. Hill himself had previously referred to these

sects as 'the lunatic fringe' of the English Revolution. Now, inspired
by the student revolt of 1968, he took them seriously, partly as a
way into the popular culture of the period, and partly as a stimulus
to fresh, 'alternative' practice in the present. 'The revolt within the
Revolution' was for Hill 'a period of glorious flux and intellectual
excitement'.[2] The radical sects of that period were not anticipating
the modern world, but working 'for something far nobler, something
yet to be achieved – the upside down world'.[3] Hill was not advocat-
ing anything so crude as direct emulation of the radical sects. For that
to happen, their modern imitators would have to take the measure
of the bizarre theology in which their practice had been embedded.
Nor did Hill gloss over the millenarian and eschatological excesses of
the sects. Nothing in that strange mental world could be treated as a
model. Hill's purpose was less prescriptive; he wanted to show that
the radical sects 'perhaps have something to say to our generation',
causing us to ponder anew on the possibilities open to us today.[4]
Repeated reprintings of *The World Turned Upside Down* suggest that
many people have been of the same view. Socially, culturally and
politically the 1640s are remote from our experience in the twenty-
first century. Yet, in that remoteness lies history's claim to tell us
something fresh about our own world.[5]

The otherness of the past

The foundation of all historical awareness is the recognition that the
past is another world; that the effect of development over time has
been to impose an ever wider gulf between ourselves and the world
of our forebears. What is manifestly true of remote ages also applies
to any period beyond the range of living memory. Already the Third
Reich is 'different' in this sense, and the world of the Cold War is
rapidly becoming so. Recognising the extent of that difference is
the first step to historical awareness. To dress our forebears in our
own clothes – as medieval artists literally did – not only commits
a visual solecism but also denies the historicity of the past. It was
the writers and artists of the Renaissance who first appreciated the
distorting effects of this kind of anachronism; but it was not until
the nineteenth century that the full implications of respecting the

integrity of the past were recognised. This was the achievement of historicism. The true historian was one who could register the full otherness of the past and who could bring it to life for contemporary readers. Today, doing history still means attempting to cross the gulf between the present and the past – a challenge to both the intellect and the imagination. What the historian expects to find on the other side is a different world.

One of the reasons why academic history stands at some distance from common understandings of the past is that popular consumption of the past tends to make it too familiar. The temptation is to populate the past with people just like us. 'Empathy' – the great rallying cry for a more accessible history in schools a generation ago – can easily mean discovering that 'they' were just like 'us', instead of getting inside a fundamentally different mentality. Accurate costuming of the past in TV documentaries and dramas means that visual anachronism is much less common than it used to be, but culture and mentality are often approached in a spirit of confident familiarity, over-adapted to the expectations of the twenty-first century.

Of course, the past is not different in every respect. Any historical encounter usually brings to light aspects of a common humanity or a shared experience, as well as the unfamiliar and bizarre. To an extent, our encounter with the past has a double-sided quality. The same time-frame may hold what is disturbingly alien and what seems reassuringly 'modern': this is a familiar feature of popular responses to ancient Athens, where ideas which are the foundation of modern philosophy took shape in a society underpinned by slavery. Proximity and distance are constantly in contention as we focus on the past; as Simon Schama has put it, 'all history is a negotiation between familiarity and strangeness'.[6] But the negotiation generally comes down on the side of strangeness. The effect of the passage of time has been to detach us ever more completely from the world of our forebears – from their material circumstances, their social arrangements, their culture and their common sense. The French historian Lucien Febvre made the point in relation to one of the material differences which can easily be overlooked – the availability of artificial light. He observed that the majority of pre-industrial people spent half their lives in total darkness. 'Can we really believe that a life of this sort fashioned in men the same mental habits and the same ways

of thinking, the same desires, the same actions and reactions as our
own life does in us?'[7] Since Febvre's day the implications of 'difference' have become progressively greater because aspects of human
experience like family and sexuality that were treated as generic or
'natural' have now been made 'strange' by being set in their historical contexts. The idea that people in the past were 'just like us' is
untenable. It is their 'obstinate unfamiliarity' which sets the terms
of understanding.[8]

Oblique illumination of the present

At first sight this strongly drawn notion of difference looks like an
unpromising foundation for applied history. It would seem to fit
more readily with the mind-set of the antiquarian, who revels in
the remoteness of the past and regards its recovery as the sole justification for scholarship. Indeed, with its call to honour the integrity
of the past, historicism seems to invite a total immersion in the relics
of the past. It is certainly true that the classical historicist position
attracts an antiquarian cast of mind. Innumerable scholarly works
have been written in which the writer is totally engrossed in the
world of the past, and oblivious to any resonance it might have
with the present. Is that not the approach which most scrupulously
respects the gulf between past and present? How can what is not only
dead and gone, but remote and sometimes alien, have any practical
bearing on today's world?

The answer is that, paradoxically, the value of the past lies precisely in what is different from our world. By giving us another
vantage point, it enables us to look at our own circumstances with
sharper vision, alert to the possibility that they might have been
different, and that they will probably turn out differently in the
future. If history could offer only a pale shadow of our own experience, it would hardly merit close examination. Instead, it opens up
other worlds with different preconceptions and different ways of
doing. At the very least, this offers a measure of detachment from
our own world; but, more than that, it allows us to evaluate our
world from another position, and thus to entertain other possibilities for its present and future development. What we aspire to, how

we organise our society and how we tackle its problems, may all be differently conceived when we turn our attention to the varied answers which have been given in the past. Thus history holds up not a mirror, but a set of counter-images. Some of those images will seem strange and irrelevant, but others may be strongly suggestive, restoring to us a perspective which has been lost for so long that it now comes with all the freshness of a discovery. Christopher Lasch was right to describe history as 'a political and psychological treasury from which we draw the reserves ... that we need to cope with the future'.[9] Seen in this light, history is not a dead weight on the present, but an intimation of possibilities. It throws the received wisdom of our age into question and promotes a healthy scepticism.

Sometimes the historical record serves as an effective reminder of a choice which has been almost completely obscured by recent developments. Today, for example, it is axiomatic that effective policing in Britain depends on tight control from Whitehall. Yet it was only with the passing of the 1964 Police Act that the Home Office secured control over local forces. Before that, in a tradition stretching back to the 1830s, the police had been subject to the authority of locally elected watch committees, which determined both policing priorities and organisational matters. It may be that the growing threat of international terrorism since 9/11 is most efficiently countered by a centralised police force, but it would make for a healthier debate if the merits of centralisation were measured against the democratic alternative which successfully operated in the past.[10]

Welfare policy, on the other hand, has proved rather more open to historical commentary – at least since Margaret Thatcher's time as Prime Minister (1979–90). But very few participants in that debate are acquainted with the history of welfare provision. Rather, they employ a limited range of reference points in the past as a means of defining more clearly what they advocate – or do not advocate – in the present. The most cited reference points are the locally controlled system of relief under the Old (i.e. pre-1834) Poor Law, the ruthless selectivity of the New Poor Law in the Victorian era, and the Beveridge Report of 1942, with its call for cradle-to-the-grave welfare. Such precedents are certainly open to rhetorical manipulation. But they also have a positive value. Each of them provides a basis for questioning the present, either by illustrating current policy in a different context, or by showing some of the implications of choosing an alternative. The Beveridge era poses the question of why a much wealthier society than he was prescribing for has qualified the principle of universal benefits. The Victorian era throws into relief the balance which should be struck between state provision and charitable provision, and it provides a sobering precedent for the 'off welfare into work' debate. The Old Poor Law shows the limits of a devolved local system of relief and highlights the family's role in supporting the poor. These earlier episodes in the history of welfare enable us to capture the peculiarity of the present, and by making possible well founded comparisons, they enlarge the pool of experience which can be drawn upon to find fresh solutions now.[11]

Perspectives for a changing world

The need for that alternative observation point on the present tends to be keenly felt during periods of rapid social change. It has been a recurrent theme in the accelerating onset of modernity in Britain since the Industrial Revolution. The clearest illustration is the Victorian fascination with the Middle Ages. This was much more than an obsession with the Gothic. Medieval society was conceived in dramatic counterpoint to the nineteenth century. For the Victorians it was characterised by stable hierarchies, close-knit communities, and a common faith reflected in a coherent aesthetic. Some Victorian evocations of the Middle Ages were romantic fantasy – like the re-staging of jousting or the fascination with courtly love. But the wider appeal of Medievalism was that it offered a perspective from which to take stock of the new world of the nineteenth century. This was one reason why historical scholarship itself gained in public standing during this period – and why so many historians specialised in the medieval period.[12] For some Victorians the Middle Ages provided not only an alternative perspective on the present, but practical means for mitigating its harshest features. Both John Ruskin and William Morris saw the medieval period in this light.

The Victorians have themselves become the object of the same retrospective critique on the present, with this difference: being only just beyond the reach of oral recall and popular memory, they are particularly subject to the fluctuating evaluation of posterity. Fifty years ago the Victorian era was perceived as different enough, but in a strongly negative light which disqualified it from illuminating the present, except to confirm the march of progress; 'the Victorians' stood for tyrannical fathers, confined wives, ground down workers and public squalor. Then, beginning in the 1950s, Victorian art and design were selectively brought within the pale of acceptable taste. Finally came the attempt by Margaret Thatcher to rehabilitate Victorian social values – or at least those of the entrepreneur. 'Victorian values' were brought into political debate as the antithesis of the Welfare State's so-called dependency culture: self-reliance, thrift and voluntarism would make the individual 'free', and at the same time provide firm foundations for national revival. Such an appeal to the past can be a positive contribution to understanding if it is open to the mixed messages that any juxtaposition of past and present throws up. The wider debates sparked by Thatcher's adoption of the Victorians certainly opened up a space in which Britain in the 1980s could be viewed from the perspective of the very different social codes which had prevailed a hundred years earlier. To that extent the Conservative discourse might be regarded as a legitimate historical exercise. But the use to which Thatcher put the Victorians shows how easily admiration for a historical period can be subordinated to a one-track agenda. It was improvised during an election campaign and subordinated to the key elements of her political philosophy – the insistence on the moral responsibility of the individual, the admiration for businessmen, and a rolling back of the state's responsibilities. Her interpretation was not open to contradiction or modification, and it was highly prescriptive: referring to Samuel Smiles, author of the 1859 bestseller *Self-Help*, Sir Keith Joseph prescribed 'a dose of Smiles' for the 'perceptible depressing limpness' in present-day individual attitudes.[13] Having noted and applauded the gap between late twentieth-century and Victorian values, Thatcher made light of all the other respects in which Victorian realities had been erased by the lapse of time. But these changes – economic, political and social – were the very reason why Victorian values were unlikely to be revived in her lifetime.[14] Given the pressures of political life, such distortions of the past are doubtless to be expected. The true value of juxtaposing past and present is more likely to be revealed by commentators who are not bound by political calculation and who are open to the different ways in which one age may illuminate another.

Recovering change over time

One of the ways in which historical difference has the capacity to take us by surprise is by overturning the belief that 'things have always been this way'. Despite the evidence of cultural diversity and adaptation all around us, many people assume that the social world they inhabit is 'natural' and therefore timeless. The historical record usually serves as a corrective to this kind of static thinking, and especially any thinking with determinist or essentialist overtones. Confident assumptions about national character or behavioural predisposition melt away when measured against the diversity of historical experience.

Black immigration into Britain is a case in point. For many years after the arrival of the *Empire Windrush* from the West Indies in 1948, black immigration was widely assumed to be an unprecedented phenomenon, with correspondingly portentous implications for the future. Historical research during the 1970s and 1980s exposed the error of this view. Mass immigration was a new development of the postwar period, but the black presence dated back to the reign of Elizabeth I. For the eighteenth century, something like a history of the black community in London proved feasible, based on documentary evidence of slaves in domestic work and freed slaves working on their own account.[15] Indeed, the pre-*Windrush* history of black people in Britain had by this time already become a political article of faith in Afro-Caribbean cultural circles. Meanwhile, among those sections of the population that were hostile to black immigration, other historical perspectives prevailed. As evidence of gross discrimination against the black minority mounted up from the time of the Notting Hill riots of 1958, whites needed an interpretation of the past which would mitigate the slur of racism. One tactic was to take cover behind the idea of the English people as a tolerant, undemonstrative and hospitable race. The inference drawn from this reading of the national character was that racial prejudice towards minorities was attributable only to a tiny and deviant element among whites.[16] Another tactic was to account for the conflict between black and white by invoking racial difference: black and white were so different, it was argued, that integration was impossible, and placing them together could only lead to bloodshed. This was the luridly pessimistic view made popular by Enoch Powell in the 1960s and 1970s, and it informed many white reactions to the inner-city riots of the 1980s. The argument was rendered more plausible by the assumption that black and white had *never* lived together in harmony – that for race relations the lesson of history was consistently negative.

Beliefs of this kind are not really historical at all, because they deny the process of change and development through time. One response of historians is to reconstruct that process, tracing the evolution of community relations since the first arrival of large numbers of immigrants (that approach is described in Chapter 3). Yet an appeal to the evidence of historical difference can often make the point more effectively: a single contrary conjuncture in the past is enough to establish that it has not 'always been thus' and to challenge the determinism in the popular view. Thus it is now clear that in the nineteenth century the supposed tolerance of the English was shown fairly sparingly towards immigrants. Competition for jobs and housing evoked strong antagonism, as the Irish knew to their cost. Strong prejudice was also shown against those groups who clung to visible cultural markers, for example the Jews from Russia. The expression of racism ranged from social 'freezing', through discrimination in the provision of services, to demands for restrictions on immigration: the Aliens Act had been passed in 1905.[17] Full-scale rioting occurred in 1919 when demobilised white soldiers and sailors attacked blacks in Liverpool and Cardiff. The historical record hardly sustains the assumption of the innate decency and hospitability of the English people.

But neither does history present an unrelieved picture of tension and violence between majorities and minorities. Eighteenth-century London provides a different perspective on relations between black and white from the one which has become entrenched through twentieth-century prejudice. London's blacks during the 1770s and 1780s numbered between 5000 and 10,000 – perhaps 0.5 per cent of the total population. The majority worked in domestic service, either as free men or as slaves brought over from the West Indies as servants. The remaining black population formed part of the urban poor, living cheek-by-jowl with whites. Slaves frequently absconded, and – to the chagrin of their masters – many vanished into the rookeries of the metropolis. This was a society where material status counted for more than ethnicity.[18] It stands as a reminder that, in any period, relations between black and white are the outcome of material circumstance and cultural belief, and that both are historically contingent.

Nostalgia and the ideal world of the past

Both the assumption of a tolerant British nation and the assumption that racial violence is inevitable make implicit inferences from history. They rest on a supposed congruence between then and now which makes light of historical difference. But contrariwise, there are also circumstances in which the gap between past and present is exaggerated in popular understanding. This is a particularly common reflex among older people in modern society who feel alienated from the pace of social change around them. They tend to experience an intense nostalgia for a vanished world – usually the world of their own parents and grandparents. They imagine the past to have been, if not a perfect world, at least a vastly preferable one, from which there has been a sad decline. Such a view is pessimistic, even fatalistic, but it can also be consoling. The historical interpretation of the past which is called into play is one in which the past is structured in opposition to the ills of the present day. It is characterised by stable family life, public decency, and trust between neighbours (as in 'the back door was never locked'). Such a past is 'different' indeed, but it depends on a highly selective reading which glosses over the negatives and simplifies the ambiguities. The gulf between past and present is artificially deepened, in order to dramatise the headlong fall from grace in the present. In this way nostalgia feeds off distorted images of the past.

Street crime is an area where the gap between popular belief about the past and the historical record is particularly clear. Every age discovers youth crime for the first time, as it were, and yearns for the supposed peace and order of the previous generation. The 1970s was a period of particularly strident alarm about street crime. The scale of street robbery was regarded as new, menacing, and un-English – a view symbolised by the American provenance of the word 'mugging', which came into common parlance for the first time. The Tory politician Sir Keith Joseph remarked that, 'for the first time in a century-and-a-half, since the great Tory reformer Robert Peel set up the Metropolitan police', parts of Britain's cities had become unsafe for peaceful citizens by night.[19] Yet over those 150 years there had been any number of comparable crime scares, when similar sentiments were uttered: the Teddy boys of the 1950s, the bag-snatchers and razor gangs of the 1930s, the original 'hooligans' of the 1890s, the 'scuttlers' of the 1880s and the 'garrotters' of the 1850s and 1860s. Each had been seen not only as a threat to life and property, but as evidence of a collapse in the national character. Street robbery may be inseparable from modern urban life, and it has certainly been a feature of British cities since at least the eighteenth century. A further distortion to bear in mind is that the scale of robbery tends to be greatly exaggerated. One crime, graphically described, is taken as symptomatic of an entire category of offence, which is then substantiated by further cases, real or rumoured. This was the pattern in 1862 when the London press reported in great detail the garrotting (i.e. choking, then robbing) of an MP on his way to his West End club. Periodically since the 1970s, mugging scares have been fanned in the same way. Thus a common feature of anxiety about street crime is that it is made to seem much more threatening than it actually is, partly by exaggerating its incidence, and partly by exaggerating its novelty. What was popularly seen as a critical marker of historical difference turns out to have shown remarkable continuity.[20]

Contemporary assumptions about child abuse also deny continuities with the past; but in this case, the obstacle is not a rose-tinted backward look, but a lack of any historical perspective at all. Since the 1989 crisis in Cleveland regarding the suspected sexual abuse of children by their parents, public anxiety has been maintained by periodic exposés of abuse of every kind. But, as Harry Ferguson has pointed out, 'one of the major effects of the recent interest in child abuse was a foreshortening of historical perspective'.[21] When the

system has failed, the media have been quick to pin the blame on the
social workers concerned. Yet failures have featured in every system
of child protection since the founding of the NSPCC in 1889. During its first 25 years the NSPCC investigated nearly 12,000 children
in the Cleveland area alone; in more recent decades the statutory
social services also built up extensive experience of such cases. The
problems of detection, protection and care which are highlighted
today are nothing new, and they raise questions far deeper than the
professional competence of individuals.[22]

The enduring and the transient

Taken together, history as difference and history as continuity provide an indispensable perspective on the present. Keeping both in
mind enables us to distinguish between what is enduring and what is
transient in our society. As Quentin Skinner has put it, 'to learn from
the past – and we cannot otherwise learn it at all – the distinction
between what is necessary and what is the product merely of our contingent arrangements, is to learn the key to self-awareness itself'.[23]
How far we differ from people in the past and how far we are the
same has considerable implications. It may affect our moral stance;
it will certainly affect our judgement about what can be jettisoned
or reformed. This was what Peter Laslett meant by 'historical sociology'. He regarded his enquiries into the seventeenth-century family
primarily as a means of 'understanding ourselves in time'. Whereas
sociologists had long assumed that pre-industrial English families
lived in extended residential families, Laslett demonstrated that
they lived in nuclear households, much like our own except for
the presence of live-in servants. This suggested to him that the
nuclear family was an entrenched feature of English society, not
likely to be superseded.[24] On the other hand, the idea of family as a
private secluded space is a much more recent development. In contemporary thinking it is often seen to be inherent in the nuclear
model, but it dates back no further than the early nineteenth century, which suggests it was much more dependent on economic and
social contingencies of the time.[25] As the distinguished American
social historian John Demos has put it,

a social problem that has always 'been there' may reasonably be regarded as intractable. But a problem that did not exist at one or another point in the past may again cease to exist in the future.[26]

To speak of a problem as 'intractable' may sound like a prescription for conservatism. But in the real world, strategies for reform require us to face up to the constraints of the past. This is not to objectify the past as a malignant force, but to recognise that patterns of behaviour which have prevailed for centuries generally meet human needs and will therefore be highly resistant to change.

If we take the measure of the radical difference of the past, we can also begin to make sense of some of the anomalies in our social and political arrangements. Many institutions and practices have a less-than-perfect fit with their current function. History usually provides the best explanation. Why do denominational schools enjoy such a high profile in our educational provision? The answer lies not in the strength of religious profession today, but in the bitter rivalries which divided Anglicans, Non-Conformists and Roman Catholics during the period 1870–1902 when the state school system was evolving.[27] Since that intense sectarianism has now disappeared, it makes little sense to defend denominational schools on grounds of tradition: their merits are better assessed by a cool look at their performance now. Equally, the royal prerogative is at odds with the principles of representative democracy. The fact that it is a survival of the feudal world, re-articulated in the seventeenth century as part of a compromise settlement between King and Parliament, should set the terms of debate about reform today. Recalling the very different circumstances in which such features developed in the past opens up the possibility of a more discriminating debate about their future.

Historical context

The gulf between our world and the past has one further implication. It is not enough to notice that a particular institution or policy takes on a different shape when traced back to an earlier point in time. Its meaning and function will be profoundly conditioned by the fact that most other aspects of the society and culture in which it is placed will be different too. In other words, the historical exists in a synchronic or horizontal dimension, as well as the more familiar vertical dimension. Knowledge about particular topics in the past should not be compartmentalised according to our categories; it must be understood in relation to the prevailing material circumstances and cultural forms of the period. In short, it is *contextual* knowledge. Of course a great deal of historical writing fails to observe this rule: one thinks of many run-of-the-mill biographies which treat the subject as an essentially modern person, rather than someone whose mentality was conditioned by the culture of the day; or, at the more academic end of the scale, economic histories which seek to apply modern economic theory to the past and hence ignore the non-economic forces which influenced economic change. But however much historians fall short of the ideal of contextual command, it remains one of the central criteria of historical scholarship.

This is a distinctive feature of the discipline of history. In the social sciences proper, like economics and sociology, the rich particularity of context tends to be subordinated to a problem-solving agenda, often driven by theory. In literary studies it is accepted by all but the more doctrinaire exponents of Postmodernism that texts cannot be understood outside their historical setting, but the effect of focusing on a single text or body of work is to impose a very limited definition of the social and the cultural context. History is unique among the disciplines in bringing every area of life and mode of thought within the scope of its enquiries. A truly historical study is one which places its object of study in the widest possible contextual frame, embracing culture, society, politics and economics. Fernand Braudel coined the phrase 'total history' to describe endeavours of this kind: his celebrated work *The Mediterranean and the Mediterranean World in the Age of Philip II* (1947) may not have successfully integrated the historical environment with the policies of the Spanish king, but it has proved a rallying call to subsequent historians.

This holistic aspect of history has important practical implications. One of the difficulties which stand in the way of grasping current issues in all their complexity is that authority is too readily granted to the technical specialist. The economist studying patterns of consumption, or the demographer analysing population trends, looks through a powerful lens, but one with a restricted field of vision which recognises only those phenomena that convention- ally fall within the scope of economics or demography. Too much policy-making is in thrall to what Hobsbawm has called 'a model of scientism and technical manipulation'.[28] Yet most problems in the modern world are inter-connected. What is most needed is the critical mind able to see the overall picture and to contextu- alise specialist knowledge in a way that bridges the conventional boundaries of 'the economic', 'the social' and so on. Historians are better able than most to take this broader view since theirs is a syn- thetic discipline, centrally concerned with linkages between areas of human activity which are usually kept discrete. It has even been claimed that a historical education equips the citizen to act as jury between rival experts. This is persuasive in principle, but it presumes a sophisticated command of the subject which would go beyond the competence of most citizens.[29] In policy-making circles, on the other hand, there is a track record of history being used effectively to offset the narrowly disciplinary perspective of technical experts. When the government convened an inter-disciplinary committee in 1986 to advise it on policy towards AIDS, Virginia Berridge recalls that it was the historians who were able to draw together the varied perspectives represented on the committee.[30]

Historical perspective can prove invaluable in breaking down the tunnel vision which easily distorts understanding of international problems. Placing these in the category of 'international relations' or 'foreign policy' without regard to context is particularly counter- productive. Retrospective analysis by historians nearly always works by broadening the context, and thus enlarging the range of fac- tors which bear on the interpretation. Thus historians no longer see the process of European imperial expansion as just an expression of maritime flair and technical superiority. They link it to economic structures, patterns of consumption, codes of masculinity and con- structions of racial difference.[31] From this perspective the media's treatment of the Gulf War in 1991 as a matter of international law and the politics of oil was manifestly inadequate.

Thinking contextually also keeps within bounds some of the most potent key words of our time. Placing particular instances under a general heading is a necessary part of gaining a purchase on the world around us. As long as the generic character of the category remains intact, there is a clear gain in understanding. But too often the definition of the category becomes skewed through the exceptional prominence accorded to particular instances. For example, the term 'genocide' is so strongly associated with the Holocaust that it tends to impose a one-dimensional meaning on highly diverse situations where mass killings have occurred. There is an urgent political and moral need to understand what happened in Rwanda and in the former Yugoslavia during the 1990s. Applying the term 'genocide' to these very diverse situations can be a hindrance to understanding; it can even lead to an unedifying attempt to rank the atrocities according to an absolute standard. Each of these tragedies requires above all a close attention to the local context of the killings and a readiness to see connections between categories we usually keep separate. Attention to context demands that we examine not just the scale of each episode, but the ideology of the perpetrators, their objectives, their methods, the degree of popular participation and approval, and the degree of resistance on the part of the victims. The differences – fully grounded in local circumstances – then become more salient than any overarching category. Thus ethnic cleansing by Serbs of Moslems in Bosnia and Kosovo displaced far more people than it eliminated; draconian though the policy was, it was hardly in the same category as the Nazi extermination of the Jews. This kind of historical specificity is a vital check on the flattening effect of a term like 'genocide' when applied to an array of different events.[32]

* * * * * * * *

Together with history as process (described in Chapter 3), history as difference expresses the essence of historical perspective. At any one time, our culture conducts dialogues with a variety of pasts. Some of those past moments confirm our sense of self by seeming to validate our values, beliefs or conventions. More often, what the past offers us is hard evidence of how our lives differ from those of our forebears. Initially the world of the past may appear strange and baffling. But once it has been understood by being placed in historical context, it becomes available for a variety of applications, all of which increase our grasp of the possibilities available in the present. It is in the very difference of the past – at first sight so distancing – that the value of history as a cultural resource lies. Only anthropology offers something comparable, but there the value of juxtaposition is diminished by a cultural and social divide which, in the case of small-scale societies typically studied by anthropologists, is too wide and too comprehensive. History offers a unique range of unexpected and illuminating insights into the present. Sometimes it enables us to come to terms with the persistence of certain historical forms; more often it opens up a hitherto unsuspected range of options. The enlightening effect of history is greatest when the difference of the past is respected, giving us the full benefit of another vantage point from which to view our own circumstances.

That experience prompts one final reflection. If the past was different from the present, the future will surely be different from the present too – separated from our world by a gulf, as surely as we are removed from the Slump of the 1930s or the high noon of Edwardian England. Any forecast founded on the belief that the next generation will follow the pattern of our own is doomed to failure. The most that can be said is that certain longstanding constraints on human action are likely to continue, and that the trajectories in which we are living may disclose the direction of cumulative change in the future.[33] Beyond that, the future is unpredictable, and one of the more certain lessons of history is that it will remain so.

3

Becoming Ourselves

When John F. Kennedy was running for President in 1960, he was asked to name his most important single asset. 'I think that it is my sense of history,' he replied. He went on to explain how vital it was to know how America had reached its present position of global influence, and beyond that 'to discern what the basic historical forces are that are moving in our own day, which ones we ought to oppose and which ones we ought to support'. For a man immersed in the minutiae of campaigning, it was a thoughtful response, reflecting a sophisticated historical mind. Kennedy saw the world as structured by continuing historical processes, in relation to which his own actions must be shaped.[1]

To think in terms of sequence or process is to think historically. Every situation which requires our understanding in the present – be it a family feud, a political upheaval or a cultural movement – is the outcome of trends and events, some of them spanning less than a lifetime, others extending back to the distant past. Today this proposition seems banal. In the heyday of historicism, however, it was a new and demanding perspective. In reaction to the rationalism and universalism of the Enlightenment, historicists asserted that the meaning of every aspect of human society was to be found in the distinctive story of its development through time. This ambitious proposition flowed directly from the first premise of historicism (explored in Chapter 2), concerning the gulf between past and present; for only by interpreting the world developmentally could the passage from 'then' to 'now' be made intelligible. History was the key to understanding the world. That was a view which received ample confirmation in different areas of nineteenth-century life. History provided the *raison d'être* of nationalism; it elevated folk-lore to a pinnacle of esteem; and it resonated with Darwin's theory of evolution.

However, during the twentieth century the standing of historicism declined sharply. The pace of technological innovation promoted a strong belief in progress, but one in which anticipation of an alluring future tended to obscure the heritage of the past. Meanwhile, in the social sciences historical explanation was eclipsed by the doctrine of functionalism, which saw social structures and patterns as parts of a working whole, best understood in relation to each other rather than as the outcome of process over time. The effect of this intellectual shift has been to diminish the cultural standing of history and historians. Because the value of the historical outlook is no longer asserted in the elevated terms that were used in the nineteenth century, it tends to be pushed to the sidelines. This explains in part why historical perspective is so under-used in public debate in Britain today. But the insights of historicism are not redundant. The historic origins of our society may not be *the* most important thing to know about it, but it cannot be denied that we are the end product of a process of becoming that only history can lay bare. It is the practical implications of this proposition with which this chapter is concerned.

Locating ourselves in history's stream

Process and development make up the habitual framework employed by historians in interpreting the past. Their object of study is not isolated events, but events in sequence. Historical change is usually seen by historians as incremental and securely moored in a sequence of development stretching back in time. While moments of total rupture are not ruled, nearly always their implied abruptness is diluted by an acute sense of the slower trajectories of change and the enduring continuities that revolution left untouched. But sequential thinking is not only the means of understanding the course of human development in the past; it also holds the clue to a critical purchase on the present. How we got from 'then' to 'now' enables us to define where we are more exactly. Thus no amount of functional analysis can account for the present position of the British monarchy: its distinctive blend of theoretical power and practical impotence, its place in the national psyche, and its phenomenal wealth, are comprehensible only as the outcome of centuries of assertion, retreat and negotiation. The case for historical understanding is even more compelling in the case of foreign policy issues. It hardly requires special pleading for a historian to assert that many of the difficulties experienced by British policy towards the former Yugoslavia during the 1990s were due to ignorance of that country's development since its creation in 1919: the wars of Yugoslav succession have been rightly called 'the last by-product of the Great War'.[2] Adequate historical briefing would have been demanding and time-consuming because the relevant history was so complex and so contested, but it was absolutely essential to formulating practicable policy goals. The need for historical depth is less obvious with regard to cultural assumptions and social behaviour, but it is just as compelling, as my examination of the history of the family in Chapter 5 will demonstrate.

Knowledge of this sort is often referred to as 'historical background'. The implication is of something left in the shadows, out of focus because it is detached from the plane of the viewer. 'Background' fails to convey the organic relationship between past and present – the sense that the present moment is no more than the point which the unfolding past has reached, and which will shortly become 'the past' also. 'Historical perspective' is much to be preferred, because it suggests that past and present are parts of a single field of vision. Where we mentally position ourselves in the past will determine our perception of the present. And not just the present: for the same angle of vision which we turn on the present can be projected into the future. Paradoxically, understanding the historical processes of the past may offer the most reliable grounds for prediction.

'Telling the story' is the first step to acquiring historical perspective. Perhaps the most basic responsibility of the historian is to ensure that the commonly accepted story corresponds with the historical facts. Stories which carry a heavy ideological load frequently fail this test, whether by omission, by outright fabrication or – more commonly – by applying an over-simplified moral yardstick to the past. In the United States until very recently, the gun culture was the subject of a largely uncontested narrative. Most Americans, so the story ran, had owned firearms since colonial days. That was what had enabled them to tame the frontier wilderness, to overcome its native inhabitants, and to take on the might of imperial Britain. The story provides the best possible grounds for defending the 'freedom' to own a gun in contemporary America. In his book *Arming America* (2000), Michael Bellesiles confronted this narrative head-on. He demonstrated that the gun culture was established much later than usually supposed. Before 1790 only 15 per cent of adult white men owned firearms, and in the Revolutionary War their role was secondary. Gun ownership only became widespread in the second half of the nineteenth century, as a result of the militarisation of society during the Civil War, and the mass production of small arms. This revised narrative had immediate political implications. If correct, it meant that gun ownership was not a founding attribute of American identity, but the by-product of the most bloody conflict in American history. It was strenuously resisted by the powerful gun rights lobby, who were able to exploit some errors that Bellesiles had made in his handling of probate records, and he was forced out of his university post. The public furore obscured the fact that Bellesiles' thesis had widespread support in the historical profession. Whether in the longer run it supplants the traditional myth of the founding frontiersman remains to be seen.[3]

In the case of Bellesiles, the political stakes could scarcely have been higher. A more mundane example can be cited from British public life. Tony Blair's plans for the reform of the National Health Service were supported by two historical assertions: first, that the NHS devised by Aneurin Bevan after the Second World War was a command bureaucracy run from Whitehall, with more than a whiff of Stalinism about it; and secondly, that hospitals in the pre-NHS 1930s reflected a cooperative and mutualist tradition, responsive to local need. The inference is that the centralised NHS should be dismantled, to be replaced by a devolved and localised structure drawing on interwar experience. But neither part of the story will stand up. According to Charles Webster, the official historian of the NHS, Bevan was explicit that the NHS should not be a top-heavy monolith, and the various reports which reviewed the NHS during the 1950s found that, far from there being over-centralisation, responsibility was devolved to the point where efficiency was compromised.[4] As for the prewar hospitals, it is true that the most prestigious were categorised as 'voluntary', in the sense of being outside local or central government control; they were funded by a variety of local contribution schemes, and they were often the object of intense local pride. But their governing bodies were neither representative nor accountable to the community; despite the big increase in mass contributory schemes between the wars, working-class subscribers had little influence on hospital policy. Central government between the wars pursued a hands-off approach towards the hospitals, and the consequence was massive inequalities of provision between different parts of the country. The 1930s hardly set a precedent for a comprehensive, locally responsive health service.[5]

Taking the story back in time

Stories like these are not an antiquarian indulgence. They are researched and remembered because they seem to explain how the present situation has come about. In theory, historical explanation is an endless ball of string, since any starting point is itself the outcome of earlier developments. A practical compromise is that the story be pushed far enough back to bring into historical focus all the key elements of the situation we are seeking to explain. That will be a good deal further back than either politicians or the public are accustomed to go. During the 1980s Ernest May and Richard Neustadt were highly effective champions of the application of history to American foreign policy. They berated successive administrations for their foreshortened historical perspective and for resorting to analogies detached from historical perspective. The essential question for decision-makers, they maintained, was 'what's the story?', and half-measures were not acceptable: the story must be traced back to the very beginning.[6] Against that standard, public understanding of many important issues is found wanting. Where the story is taken to have begun can make a very substantial difference to how the present is read.

Consider, for example, the issue of Israel–Palestine. Much depends on how the conflict is read by those states which are in a position to help or hinder its resolution – principally the United States. Since they became drawn into serious diplomacy in the region during the 1980s, the Americans have consistently taken the base-line to be the Six-Day War of 1967. What is up for negotiation is the withdrawal of Israel's boundaries from the full extent of the 1967 annexations. Of course, this has a close bearing on the shape of any future Palestinian state, but it is not the Palestinians' central concern. For them, the defining moment in modern history was not 1967, but 1948, when 250,000 Palestinians were expelled from Israel: this was 'the catastrophe' (*al-Nakba*). As Ilan Pappe has pointed out, understanding of the Israel–Palestine problem is drastically distorted if the base-line is set too recently.[7] The full measure of the conflict can only be taken if the formative experience of 1948 is incorporated into the story.

An example closer to home is the role of trade unions in Britain. Popular estimation of the unions today is conditioned by the severely constricted part they have played during the past twenty years, and by the memory of the bruising industrial conflicts with Tory governments in the 1970s and 1980s. A narrative structured along these lines has the effect of denying the historic importance of the unions in British society. Alastair Reid's recent history *United We Stand* (2004) aims to correct this impression. He traces the evolution of the unions back to the early nineteenth century, and documents their struggles to win the right to organise, the right to representation and the right to work. All of these are integral to almost any definition of civil liberties, yet none of them is a completed agenda. Nor has their progressive realisation been a smooth trajectory. To take two well-known instances: in the early nineteenth century the Combination Acts inhibited union organisation until their repeal in 1824; and for five years after the Taff Vale judgement of 1901 the unions were liable for huge damages arising from industrial action. Against this background Reid considers that the unions may well grow in membership and influence in the coming years, particularly if near-full employment is maintained. In the 1880s the character of British trade unions was changed by the recruitment of a large pool of hitherto unionised labour, much of it unskilled and supporting a more radical set of demands: this was the 'new unionism'. Reid observes that there is another such pool today, concentrated in the service industries, which may reinvigorate the trade unions in the future. Many politicians and much of the media today have an interest in drastically foreshortening the story so that it corresponds with popular assumptions about the unions. All the more reason to insist, as Reid does, that the starting point be pushed back well beyond its conventional beginning.[8]

The idea of taking the story back to its beginning is a useful corrective to the dangers of foreshortened narrative, but it needs to be carefully qualified. The analogy with a story suggests that, in hindsight at least, the content of the narrative is self-evident, allowing no room for debate about what should be included. Yet any narrative which bears explanatory weight invites just such a debate, to the point where it may make more sense to think in terms of several stories converging at one point. The attack on the Twin Towers in New York in September 2001 presented a striking example. In the American reaction there was initially space for no more than overwhelming feelings of outrage and vengeance. But once attention turned to the forming of a rational response, historians had an important contribution to make. Fred Halliday pointed out that the attack only made sense when it was seen as a convergence of a number of processes, not all of which had previously been considered together: the growth of Islamic fundamentalism (linked to notions of *jihad*); the continuing crisis in Palestine; the collapse of central power in several Islamic countries; the resentment against US intervention in the Middle East, especially since the Gulf War; and the instability of international relations since the end of the Cold War.[9] There was not one story to unravel, but several.

The sanction of the past

Telling the story, especially in abbreviated form, may also convey a misleading idea of a smooth, almost pre-ordained route to the present. From this it can be a small step to regarding today's institutions as hallowed by their past and to be defended against suggestions of reform or radical change. This is most strikingly the case in pre-literate societies, which often treat origins as a sacred charter, whose content serves to authenticate present-day institutions: what the ancestors created is what exists today. But the enlistment of history to reinforce the social order is certainly not confined to small-scale societies. It has been a marked feature of many modernising societies, including Britain, where validating the political institutions of the country became crystallised as the 'Whig interpretation' of history. Victorian historians of the English constitution (many of them aligned with the Whig or Liberal Party) regarded Parliament as the benign fulfilment of a centuries-long process of development – from the Anglo-Saxon *witenagemot* through Simon de Montfort to the Glorious Revolution of 1688. One of the reasons why Parliament was viewed with such reverence in the nineteenth century was that this extended pedigree was common knowledge.[10] In this narrow sense the Whig interpretation has little currency today. Yet a comparable reflex is at work in accounting for popular attachment to the monarchy (as distinct from the Royal Family).

Invoking the sanction of the distant past in this way is completely at odds with the notion of historical process. The historian's interest in beginnings is not that they disclose the shape of the present, but that they mark a convenient point from which to track a sequence of changes which cumulatively may account for the present. But even without an exaggerated respect for origins, hindsight tends to cast the narrative in a more coherent shape than was actually the case, identifying a sequence of developments which 'lead up to' the present. The historical record seldom bears out this picture. It highlights errors, false starts and reversals, as much as grand projects brought to fruition. Above all, it brings to the fore contingency. In the guise of the role of 'accident' in history this has been a hardy perennial of historiographical debate for a long time. It is more helpful to think of contingency as an intrusive incident which does not 'belong' to the story, but which affects its development – like the unexpected death of a statesman, or the arrival of a pandemic. The impact of contingency explains one of the recurrent themes of history, namely the inability of historical actors to anticipate the later development of the story they are part of. Simon Szreter calls this the 'prospective indeterminacy of the past'. He instances economic growth in industrial Britain as a 'crooked path' – or a potholed road – which no one in their right mind would want to emulate.[11]

Pointing out the twists and turns disposes of the notion that there was a pre-ordained path. But there was still a path taken. Today's world was never planned, but it is nevertheless the outcome of processes which have unfolded over time, and it is part of the historian's task to expose them to view. Hence to see the world as only the outcome of contingency is no less distorted than to see it as the working out of a grand scheme. There has recently been a vogue for 'virtual' or counterfactual history, in which historians reconstruct what would have happened if some critical event had not taken place ('if Napoleon had won the battle of Waterloo'). This is not quite so perverse as it sounds. Niall Ferguson has thought through the implications more carefully than most. His consideration of alternatives or counterfactuals is restricted to those which had currency among people of the time, allowing 'how it actually wasn't' to inform our understanding of what happened. In answer to the question 'What would have happened if Britain had "stood aside" in August 1914?', Ferguson predicts that Germany would have won the war and created a German version of the European Union; meanwhile Britain, spared the exhaustion of four years' blood-letting, would have been in a stronger position to stand up to German hegemony today. Yet most of Ferguson's essay is given over to analysing the widely divergent British strategies for dealing with Germany at the time, culminating in the bitter divisions within the Asquith government on the eve of the war. This procedure has the merit of showing that British intervention was far from inevitable, but at the cost of elevating contingency to a disproportionate explanatory role.[12]

Divergent time-scales

Practical understanding of historical processes which are manifest in the present also has to come to terms with the fact that their time-scales are markedly divergent. Some of the threads in international relations today need be traced back only to the pulling down of the Berlin Wall in 1989; popular accounts of British welfare politics take as their starting point the Beveridge Report in 1942, though the more thorough ones take the story back to the introduction of old age pensions in 1908; modern fertility patterns invite a perspective dating back to the 1860s; arable land-usage in England, to the eighteenth century; the role of the Anglican Church as the established church, to the sixteenth century; and so on. In each case the past – and sometimes the remote past – conditions aspects of the present. Earlier epochs have all left residues in the present. Indeed, one of the tasks of revisionism is to push the relevant antecedents further back than was commonly supposed. Thus the Iron Curtain which divided Western from Eastern Europe after 1945 was more than an expression of rivalry between the Great Powers; it also reflected a cultural divergence which began to develop when the administration of the Roman Empire was divided between East and West in the third century AD. The processes of history do not march in step, but according to different time-scales. Indeed, distinguishing between these time-scales was elevated into a theory of history by Fernand Braudel, the scholar who dominated the *Annales* school of historians in France during the postwar era. Braudel saw history unfolding in three registers: underpinning all else was structural history, an almost motionless framework of environmental constraints, but also including slow-moving cultural forms, 'little touched by the obstinate erosion of time'.[13] The second tier was the history of conjunctures, which Braudel defined as movements in economics or demography over a cycle of ten to fifty years. The conventional subject-matter of the political historian belonged to the third level, *l'histoire événementielle*, flaring up in the night like 'a firework display of phosphorescent fireflies' and briefly illuminating the landscape around it. Braudel called these three levels 'the plurality of social time'.[14] Historical processes have sometimes been marked by abrupt transitions when history, as it were, speeded up. At the other extreme, history may almost stand still, its flow only perceptible with the hindsight of many centuries. This may sound overly schematic. But, for Braudel, the integration of these different rhythms into a single analysis was the aim of history (even if his own success was qualified). His quarrel with sociology was precisely that it did not have the means to combine structural analysis with the play of events.[15]

One of the main reasons why the present so often seems contradictory and incoherent is because what we observe or experience is marked by the residue of different historical levels. Each generation is characterised by an incongruous mixture of old and new, which

lends itself to faulty readings. Full-time regular employment has
often been assumed to be the historic norm of British society. The
reality was exposed in 1991 by Noel Whiteside in a book published
in the 'Historical Handbooks' series.[16] At that time the typical British
man was still taken to be the full-time worker on fixed hours, who
was not only comparatively well paid but also received a range of
benefits, from occupational pensions to protection against unfair
dismissal. Yet, as Whiteside showed, full-time work of this kind
dated back only to the introduction of factory production during
the Industrial Revolution. It had grown steadily as mechanisation
expanded during the nineteenth century, until by the time of the
First World War it was treated as the norm by unions and employers
alike. But since the 1970s the trend had been the other way, as part-
time employment rapidly expanded. Whiteside's point was that for
as long as full-time work with fixed hours is taken to be the norm,
the generality of workers will not be treated equitably or rationally.
Fifteen years on, and despite some reform, the structure of benefits
still reflects the outdated picture she described in 1991. That is likely
to continue until full-time work is seen for what it is – a relatively
recent and historically contingent development.[17]

Correcting a mistaken impression of antiquity can have major
political consequences. In the southern states of the USA in the
1950s most whites believed that racial segregation had existed for
time out of mind – as far back as the age of slavery. The historian C. Vann Woodward wrote *The Strange Career of Jim Crow* to
demonstrate how far this was from the truth. Most of the relevant
legislation – the so-called Jim Crow laws – dated no further back than
the late nineteenth century, and there had been black members of
the Congress and black locally elected officials in the same period.
Woodward did not deny that important features of segregationist
practice – for example, in the churches, the schools and the army –
went back much earlier. What he disputed was that a comprehensive
system of segregation had 'always' existed in the South, and that it
could never be changed.[18] Martin Luther King called Woodward's
book 'the historical Bible of the civil rights movement', yet this was
no partisan rhetoric, but a careful historical exposition.[19]

Sometimes all talk of a dynamic relation between past and present
seems beside the point: the world is being created anew, and the

function of the past is reduced to providing an antiquarian escape from the brave new world or its double image, the terrible new dawn: 1945 was such a moment. The historian Alan Bullock has recalled his belief that the disappearance of a united Germany, the emergence of two new superpowers, and the dropping of the atom bomb meant an irreparable break with the past.[20] A generation later, as memory of the immediate postwar world had faded, another new beginning was signalled by the coming down of the Berlin Wall in 1989, swiftly followed by the collapse of Communism and the end of the Cold War. Historians are sometimes charged with being obsessed with continuity – with tracing so much to its antecedents that all sense of new turnings is lost.[21] It is true that, confronted by a major turning point in the past, the historian will look backwards for trajectories and portents. But that is because 'the new' is never a clean slate; it brings together elements from the past in new circumstances and in a new relation to one another. As Bullock went on to point out, old patterns began to reassert themselves almost immediately after 1945.[22] 'The new' is never new in an absolute sense: it is the new acting on the past, and vice versa. Drawing those kinds of distinction is one of the most illuminating contributions the historian can make.

Globalisation in perspective

The argument of this chapter can best be illustrated by placing in perspective a key feature of the contemporary world, generally presumed to be without precedent. Globalisation is the modernising rhetoric of our age *par excellence*. It conveys a world drastically shrunk in time and distance, so that goods, services and ideas may find their level in a global market-place. To the economist, globalisation points to an ideal scenario in which capital flows, labour market, production and consumption are perfectly integrated into a single world system. In cultural terms, globalisation is a mélange of disparate elements drawn from different parts of the world but increasingly homogenised into a standard product. Whether applauded or reviled, globalisation has become the defining feature of the contemporary world. Assertions to this effect often carry the implication that globalisation is entirely new.[23] If that is so, then the lessons of history are likely to be severely limited. If, on the other hand, 'globalisation' is merely the modern name for a centuries-long process, it would be foolish to turn our backs on the insights the historical perspective offers.

'Globalisation' is the appropriate term to refer to a world where the leading commercial powers practise free trade, where their currencies are held in stable exchange rates, where there is uncontrolled inter-continental migration, and where up-to-date systems of communication are being extended to every corner of the globe. This list has a resoundingly modern ring, yet only the last feature applies to the world in 2007. Most of the G8 countries apply protection to their key products; the currency markets are dysfunctionally volatile; and migration is fiercely controlled. That description in fact refers to the world in about 1870. The leading industrialised and industrialising countries then subscribed to the free trade system advocated by Britain. All their currencies were convertible at a fixed rate against gold. There was large-scale free migration from Europe to the Americas, as well as directed migration from India and China to Africa and the Caribbean. The telegraph was cutting down communication times from weeks to hours, while the steam ship was enhancing the speed and comfort of passenger travel. The business cycle had become truly global in its range, the first slumps occurring in 1857 and 1873. Eric Hobsbawm's brilliant depiction of this period is appropriately titled 'the world unified'.[24] 'High globalisation' is the label that economic historians apply to the later nineteenth century, but which they are reticent in applying to the present.[25] The comparison between 1870 and the present brings out two points. First, globalisation has not sprung like a new phenomenon from the postwar economic boom, or from the collapse of Communism after 1989. It is a long-term process, in which what seems new today often amounts to no more than an increase in degree beyond what existed a generation ago. Secondly, globalisation is always uneven, more fully realised in some spheres than in others. Those who celebrate globalisation today might well feel chastened as they reflect on the free labour market 130 years ago.

Globalisation is often identified with an expansive Western capitalism drawing into its orbit a number of discrete traditional cultures and giving them access to the global networks they had never had before. What this overlooks is the record of those same cultures in constructing wide-ranging commercial and cultural networks before the Europeans had stirred beyond their coastal horizons. The late fifteenth century – the period of Vasco da Gama and Columbus – marked the beginning of European long-haul oceanic trade, but its significance in the history of globalisation is not so cut-and-dried. Prior to the sixteenth century it was China and Islam whose commerce and culture approximated closest to a global reach. In a work of truly global scholarship, C. A. Bayly points out that there was little to choose between the European states and a host of contemporary polities ranging from Qing China to the Ottoman Turks: all were predominantly agrarian, and all had extensive trading networks; Bayly calls this 'archaic globalisation'.[26] Only in the course of the eighteenth century did the more aggressive imperialism of the Atlantic states shift the balance decisively away from the great land powers of Asia. The 1760s – when the British became a major land power in India – has been dubbed by one historian 'the globalizing decade'.[27] The Atlantic slave economy was also at its height at this time. The growing of sugar cane by African slaves in the Caribbean was the lucrative activity on which a complex web of ancillary trade turned. Cowries were shipped from the Maldives to serve as a medium of exchange in West Africa; the slaves were fed on cod fished in the Newfoundland waters; they worked the soil with tools manufactured in England; and they wore clothes woven in New England. Thousands of British investors, both large and small, had a stake in the slave trade. The profits of that trade, and of the plantation system itself, added significantly to the country's capital stock, to the benefit of its industry, its agrarian improvement and its urban amenities. Coercion was a continuing feature of globalisation during the nineteenth century, the climax of empire. Britain used force to impose free trade and an open road for British investment on many weaker societies from West African coastal chiefdoms to the Chinese Empire, behind a globalising rhetoric of internationalism and freedom.

Last but not least, the period between 1870 and the mid-twentieth century ought to have a special claim on the attention of globalisation specialists because it demonstrates that globalisation, like any other historical process, can be knocked off course. Both the First and the Second World War brought the principal institutions of globalisation to a grinding halt. Britain, the dynamic force behind nineteenth-century globalisation, was financially brought low by the Depression. Germany and Japan moved sharply away from a liberal economic system, adopting instead policies of economic autarky. State-led protectionism was the order of the day. Globalisation presumes a steady growth in world trade and capital flows, but between 1930 and 1950 they went into reverse, not recovering 1913 levels until the 1980s. This was 'de-globalisation' with a vengeance.[28]

A cataclysmic reverse of these proportions is regarded as an unlikely eventuality by most analysts today. There is perhaps more food for thought in the vicissitudes of the international economic system between 1880 and 1914. This was the period when the global future seemed most assured, but internal contradictions and popular pressure forced a significant slow-down. In the first place, France, Germany and the United States introduced protective tariffs. Confronted by the continuing economic lead of Great Britain, these countries were no longer moved by the argument that all stood to gain by the free market. They were reacting against its unequal distributional consequences, in what has been aptly termed a 'globalization backlash'.[29] Secondly, the free international movement of labour began to be eroded. The United States, Canada, Mexico, Argentina and Brazil all took their first steps in limiting the numbers of immigrants, becoming more restrictive after the First World War.

None of this history is inaccessible or only very recently researched, but it scarcely features in the public debate on globalisation, partly because it exposes the self-serving contradictions of the Western agenda.[30] For affluent societies fearful of 'swamping' by immigrants from poor countries, the free international labour market that was partly realised in the nineteenth century is much too subversive a thought. Also forgotten is the historic association of globalisation with coercion.[31] To dwell on that might turn the spotlight on the behind-the-scenes pressure that the leading capitalist powers exert on less developed countries, either bilaterally or through multilateral world agencies. Finally, the 'modernising' policies recommended to those countries completely contradict the experience of the most developed countries. Top of the list is free trade, widely seen as the key to development. Yet the majority of advanced capitalist economies followed the opposite path. They knew that their infant industries could only be nurtured by protection and set their tariffs accordingly. This was true of the USA for most of the nineteenth century, France and Germany in the latter part of the century, and the Asian tigers after 1945. It was even true of Britain itself during the critical take-off period before 1846. Free trade was the preferred system for Britain once its industrial lead was comfortably secure, not while it was an apprentice. In requiring less developed countries to adopt free trade policies, the developed world is asking them to 'kick away the ladder', as Ha-Joon Chang has aptly put it, and thus reinforce its own ascendancy.[32]

It is therefore a half-truth to say that globalisation is new. Of course there are palpably new elements, especially in the technology of communications (though it is worth recalling that the same was true of the 1870s). But the implications of globalisation – and its future prospects – can only be grasped if it is understood as the latest stage in a centuries-long process. That record speaks again and again of the contradiction between the emollient rhetoric of globalisation and its often ruthless operating methods. The skewed and self-serving history lesson given to less developed countries in the name of economic progress is only the latest instance of this. Viewing globalisation with extended hindsight offers another lesson in realism: the continuing integration of the world is highly likely, but only over the long term; in the short term, globalisation may falter or even go into reverse. As two economic historians of the late nineteenth century put it, 'the record suggests that unless politicians worry about who gains and who loses, they may be forced by the electorate to stop efforts to strengthen global economy links, and perhaps even to dismantle them'.[33] Globalisation, then, far from being 'outside history', turns out (as is so often the case with presumed novelty) to be a prime candidate for practical historicism.

Globalisation is a good example of the way in which interpretations of the past are inextricably linked with projections into the future. Historical processes are trajectories which not only help to explain the present but may also disclose what lies ahead. We feel

confident in predicting a continuing revolution in global communications because the forces which produced that revolution over
the past generation are still strong and give no sign of diminishing: the build-up of top-quality research in electronics over the past
thirty years, and the continuing popular appetite for ever faster and
ever more flexible modes of communication. One might give added
depth to the prediction by citing the earlier nineteenth-century
sequence of railway, steamship, telegraph and telephone as evidence
that improving communications is a defining attribute of modern
capitalist society – then, now and in the future.

The limits of prediction

Prediction is the most contentious dimension of applied history.
The wider audience for history probably regards prediction as the
most useful practical function historians could perform, and it feels
let down by their failure to oblige. The reticence of historians is
hardly surprising, given that predicting the future is the precise
opposite of what they spend their lives doing. When historians do
gaze into their crystal ball, the results have often been embarrass-
ing. In 1988 Paul Kennedy wrote a bestseller designed to uncover
the dynamic of rise and decline among the world's great powers by
setting them against their predecessors. After noting the continuing
stagnation of the Soviet economy, he remarked that this 'does not
mean that the USSR is close to collapse' – an unfortunate judgement,
given the rapid unravelling of the Soviet Union between 1989 and
1992.[34] He also urged Americans to face up to an imminent decline
from global dominance, which has still not materialised twenty
years later. The record is little better in economic history, despite
the pronounced cyclical tendency in the sequence of boom and
recession. Few economic historians predicted the economic crisis of
1973, which brought to an end the 25-year boom after the Second
World War.

One reaction on the part of historians to these failures is to withdraw from prediction altogether, and to see the present as the full
extent of what historians can explain. At the height of the Vietnam
War, when both its supporters and its opponents were much given

to prediction, Arthur Schlesinger observed that history makes us understand 'the extreme difficulty, the intellectual peril, the moral arrogance of supposing that the future will yield itself so easily to us'; in the last analysis, history was 'inscrutable'.[35] This was not quite the passive stance it sounds. Schlesinger was not just urging historians to refrain from prediction; he wanted the public to come to a realistic sense of the inaccessibility of the future. Alan Bullock took a similar view. History is littered with well-informed predictions by intelligent people who turned out to be wrong. Bullock maintained that the lesson to be learned from this sorry record is to be mentally prepared for surprises.[36] Counterfactual history – the study of 'what might have happened' – with its heavy emphasis on the fickleness of events, tends towards the same conclusion.[37] Maturity comes through accepting the unpredictability of the future and rejecting the illusion of prophecy.

But historians can offer more than this. Anyone who makes predictions of detail or timing is unlikely to be vindicated, since these are the areas where contingency has most scope. But the processual or linear mode of thinking engages with history at a different level. It identifies trajectories that can be verified in the present and which are likely to continue in the future; the specifics of time and place are beside the point. Important features may be modified, and the cast of characters may change, but the general path is clear. The twentieth-century history of South Africa provides a striking instance. During the 1970s and 1980s most observers concluded that it would only be a matter of time before majority rule came about, even though the *apartheid* regime was then at its most entrenched. No doubt that view was influenced by revulsion against the excesses of white rule, and by the political maturity of the black resistance. But what gave it added conviction was the triumphant record of African nationalism. By 1980, South Africa was the sole white minority regime in the entire continent; all other countries were governed in the name of the majority. A historical process appeared to be awaiting completion. Within South Africa, organised African resistance dated back to the foundation of the South African Natives National Congress (later the ANC) in 1912: its time would surely come. What could not be predicted was the manner of emancipation, whether by revolution from below, or by timely devolution from above, or some combination of the two (as actually transpired). But although substantial details remained obscure, the broad lineaments of the future were clear.

* * * * * * * *

As E. H. Carr explained, a prediction of revolution, if it has any value at all, must be based on the history of the country concerned. The historian can point to the likelihood – even the probability – of revolution, but cannot say when that will be. The fact that the revolution will be realised through the occurrence of unique events which cannot be predicted, does not invalidate the prediction.[38] Carr might have added that neither could a straight road to revolution be presumed. The crooked path which so often obscures the route taken in the past will very likely obscure the route to be taken in the future. Valid predictions, then, are those which extrapolate from an extended historical trend, which address big collective themes, and which do not specify a fixed time-scale. Hardly the crystal ball, but a useful purchase on the future none the less. Beyond that, understanding how we got from 'then' to 'now' gives us some grasp of where our world has come from. It reveals the stories in which our lives continue to be embedded. And it suggests how initiatives for change in today's generation may be facilitated or frustrated by the inheritance of the past.

4

Parallels in the Past

Historical analogy is the most common kind of applied history. Politicians rely on examples drawn from the past, and political issues are often presented to the public in the same way. Some analogies serve to commend a particular course of action; others point a cautionary moral. Margaret Thatcher's re-thinking of the social security system was attacked as a return to the means-test of the 1930s, and even as a throw-back to the harsh philosophy of the New Poor Law of 1834. The British National Party, like the National Front before it, is routinely portrayed as a return to Oswald Mosley's Blackshirts in the 1930s. Such instances could be multiplied. At first glance they imply a public well acquainted with the historical approach to current affairs. The problem is that the most popular analogies are at odds with the principles of historical reasoning. Indeed, since historical perspective is defined in terms of the twin concepts of process and difference, analogical reasoning would appear to be entirely invalid. Invoking our predecessors' experience as a guide to conduct all too easily overlooks the difference between their circumstances and ours; it also discounts the processes of change and development which have taken place in the meantime. For these reasons, analogy is routinely condemned as profoundly unhistorical by the gate-keepers of the academy. For Keith Thomas, the difference between modern and pre-modern historical sensibilities is that we study the past in order to experience its difference, whereas our forebears expected it to furnish lessons.[1] G. R. Elton, while conceding that analogies may have value in prompting new lines of enquiry, insists that they prove nothing.[2] David Hackett Fischer, in his survey of the historian's fallacies, offers a more discriminating rebuttal. He concedes the possible merit of using the present to illuminate the past, but rejects the reverse procedure as 'dangerous both to logic and to empiricism'.[3]

If by 'analogy' we mean an *assumption* of correspondence or equivalence, then these strictures are justified. Historical awareness is indeed profoundly hostile to the idea that one situation can be read in terms of another separated by the lapse of years: past and present are, by definition, different worlds. But analogical reasoning does not rest on a presumption of complete congruence or repetition. The word itself denotes comparison of a more open-ended kind. All human beings engage in almost continuous analogical reasoning as a means of finding their bearings in constantly changing circumstances. Most of the time we do not look for absolute repetition; we refer to our previous experience as much to establish what the present is *not*, as to confirm what it *is*. All that an analogy lays down is that 'if two or three things agree in one respect, then they might also agree in another'.[4] The whole point of an analogy is that it notes similarities in things which in other respects are unalike. A perfect analogy – usually taken to mean complete congruence – is a contradiction in terms.

By 'analogical thinking', then, I mean any use of the past which departs from the sequential mode and sets up a comparison with some episode or set of circumstances in the past. What historical analogy typically reveals is both contrast and convergence. Provided we are open to both, the effect is to liberate our thinking from the rigidities of current discourse, not by prescribing a course of action, but by expanding our sense of the options. The argument of this chapter is that, contrary to most statements on the subject, historical analogy can be an aid to critical thinking. But first, due acknowledgement must be made of the pitfalls of simplistic analogical reasoning.

The long memories of statesmen

In October 1962 during the Cuba missiles crisis, John F. Kennedy reflected on his reading of Barbara Tuchman's recently published

The Guns of August, a best-selling account of how the Great Powers stumbled into world war in 1914. He told his brother Robert:

> I am not going to follow a course which will allow anyone to write a comparable book about this time, *The Missiles of October*. If anybody is around to write after this, they are going to understand that we made every effort to find peace and every effort to give our adversary room to move.[5]

Analogy counts for a lot in international relations. Foreign policy resembles a narrative of conflict, accommodation and cooperation, an ongoing drama often featuring the same cast, with the addition of new players who must be assimilated into the existing mental framework. Foreign countries are viewed as actors with motives and prejudices extending back beyond the time of the politicians who are actually in power. In relation to the USA or France, for example, the British establishment is not merely dealing with the current president and his administration, but is playing the latest scene in a story which extends back to the Second World War, with many critical points along the way, each of which may strike a resonance now. When a crisis suddenly materialises and quick responses are needed, analogies often provide the easiest way of getting a purchase on the situation. The burden of precedent is intensified by the way in which events in international relations are personalised, with credit and blame attributed to the statesmen involved. Popular knowledge reflects these features in simplified form: in common currency the history of international relations comprises a limited number of critical moments from which the nation emerged with credit or infamy. There is still mileage to be obtained from comparing a British politician to Neville Chamberlain or Winston Churchill. This compounds the politicians' awareness of the precedents against which they in turn will be judged. In looking over his shoulder at August 1914, Kennedy was anticipating an invidious comparison which would have tarnished his reputation had the missile crisis not been peacefully resolved.

Another statesman much exercised by analogies with 1914 was François Mitterrand. As the Bosnian crisis deepened in 1992, the elderly French president travelled to Sarajevo not only to see the situation for himself, but to dramatise the danger that this Balkan conflict might escalate and draw in other powers. That was why he made the journey on 28 June, the anniversary of Gavrilo Princip's assassination of the Archduke Franz Ferdinand in the same city. As Eric Hobsbawm pointed out, the failure of the international press to pick up the allusion to 1914 demonstrated that the outbreak of the First World War was now too remote to feature as part of public memory (though the same could not be said of the war itself, which still functions as a shorthand for pointless slaughter). Mitterrand was attempting to draw on a historical analogy which by 1992 had passed out of use.[6]

The appeasement analogy

The Second World War, on the other hand, is still very much part of public memory, especially the belief that it could have been avoided if the politicians had only been more perceptive and more courageous. That view was strongly advocated after the war by Winston Churchill, especially in the first volume of his war memoirs, *The Gathering Storm*.[7] In the public mind there is probably greater clarity about the precipitants than about the events of the war itself. 'Appeasement' is a term which really only has one historical referent, and it remains one of the more wounding insults in the political lexicon. For the generation who had lived through the 1930s and who rose to the top between the 1950s and the 1970s, parallels with the appeasement era were inescapable.

It may seem surprising that the country most preoccupied by the analogy of appeasement was not directly involved in the run-up to war in 1939: the United States took a firmly isolationist stance in international affairs throughout the interwar period. But for a country conducting a global foreign policy for the first time, historical precedent was particularly important. American policy during the Cold War, it has been argued, was obsessed with analogies.[8] The rhetoric of appeasement was not only a means of promoting policy decisions to a public familiar with this reading of the 1930s; it also conditioned the thinking of the policy-makers themselves. On at least two occasions the precedent of appeasement influenced

American foreign policy. When North Korea invaded South Korea in 1950, Harry S. Truman placed the North in the same category as the Japanese, Italians and Germans in the 1930s. In deploying American troops in Korea he aimed to halt the Communists in their tracks, and thus to avoid the supposed weakness displayed by Western leaders in the face of Hitler and Mussolini.[9] Truman was explicit about the importance of historical analogy: as he later recalled,

> I had trained myself to look back in history for precedents, because instinctively I sought perspective in the span of history for the decisions I had to make. That is why I read and re-read history.

For Truman and his advisors, the 1930s were the most vivid period in history.[10]

The debate was reprised fifteen years later in the Johnson administration during the run-up to the Vietnam War. Once again, the behaviour of a Communist adversary was interpreted in terms set by earlier crises: Korea and Munich were the most important. Officials maintained that the world was experiencing a repetition of the dangers posed by the dictators thirty years before, and that World War III was in prospect unless they took decisive action. The 'domino theory', which predicted that other countries would quickly fall under Communist control if South Vietnam succumbed, drew explicitly on Central Europe's experience of Nazi expansion in the 1930s. As President Johnson put it in 1965,

> Nor would surrender in Viet-Nam bring peace, because we learned from Hitler at Munich that success only feeds the appetite of aggression. The battle would be renewed in one country and then another country, bringing with it perhaps even larger and crueller conflict, as we have learned from the lessons of history.[11]

Even today, nearly seventy years after Munich, appeasement has not lost its place in political arguments in favour of pre-emptive war. We do not yet know whether the Munich analogy featured strongly in the discussions of the British Cabinet on the Iraq crisis in 2002–3, but ministers did not hesitate to deploy it in their speeches and articles. In February 2003, Tony Blair compared his opponents to those who 'saw no need to confront Hitler'.[12] It was hardly necessary for him to make the point since it was repeated *ad nauseam* in the British press.

The problem with the appeasement analogy is that it tends to be given privileged status over any other precedent. During the debates preceding American action in Korea and Vietnam – and again when the British were preparing for action in Suez – the argument for intervention rested on a single parallel which acquired the status of a prescription. Provided there was a threat to the status quo or to a friendly nation, 'Munich' appeared to provide a certain guide. As Cyril Buffet and Beatrice Heuser have pointed out, this kind of analogy imposes a monocausal analysis: if the dictator is not compelled to retreat, there will be war.[13] No other outcomes could be considered within this frame. Nor was allowance made for the intervening processes of historical change, which made the world of the 1950s and 1960s a very different place from that of the 1930s. It was almost impossible for analysts to take seriously the yawning differences between Central Europe in the 1930s and the Far East in the 1950s and 1960s. Features which were highly specific to the 1930s were treated as general truths. In the case of the analogy between Vietnam and Munich, little account was taken of the disparity between the Vietcong and the Sudeten Germans, or between American military strength and the under-prepared British and French forces in 1938.[14] The logic of the analogy was that Ho Chi Minh was 'another Hitler': he was assimilated to the model of evil dictator, rather than understood as the product of a specific time and place.[15] This had the serious consequence of closing the official mind to the full complexity of the current crisis. In both Korea and Vietnam the Americans failed to grasp the motives of their antagonist, or to gauge the likely consequences of going to war – which in each case went far beyond what had been anticipated. It is hard to avoid the conclusion that precedents from the appeasement era were invoked in order to confirm a prior conviction and foreclose argument.[16]

However, 'Munich' is a very specific kind of historical analogy. During the postwar era it expressed an overwhelming consensus about the causes of the greatest disaster in living memory, and about the compelling need to avoid its repetition. It was viewed not so much as a take-it-or-leave-it lesson, but as a profound 'truth'. Because 'Munich' highlighted the responsibility that the leaders of Britain and France had borne for the outbreak of war in 1939, it placed their successors in a moral straitjacket. Those who counselled caution or accommodation vis-à-vis the Communist powers were at risk of being placed in the same category as 'the men of Munich'. 'Munich' was thus *the* historical reference point in international relations – justly described as 'the most powerful and influential political myth of the second half of the twentieth century'.[17] The more hegemonic an analogy, the more likely it is to stand in the way of understanding the present. In dictating a single perspective it imposes a tunnel vision.

Open-ended analogies

The real merits of analogical thinking become evident in cases which are not morally over-determined, and which do not impose a mono-causal approach. Once those conditions are removed, the effect of drawing a historical analogy is more likely to highlight differ-ences than similarities. The contrast between 'then' and 'now' is valuable because it makes possible a better grasp of what is distinc-tive about the present. The postwar reconstruction of Iraq is a case in point. As the troops moved in, US officials made light of the post-pacification problems which lay ahead by citing the astonish-ing progress Japan had made under American tutelage after 1945. In a paper entitled 'Don't Expect Democracy This Time', John W. Dower points out that – unlike in Iraq in 2003 – the Americans had enjoyed a number of specific advantages in Japan. Having made an unconditional surrender, the Japanese accorded a degree of legiti-macy to the occupying forces, while neighbouring countries were frankly relieved that Japan was under foreign occupation. The tran-sition was facilitated by the ousted emperor's deft cooperation with the new regime. The American reconstruction of Japan represented the final fling of New Deal idealism, for example in land reform and labour law. Lastly, because Japan possessed no strategic raw mate-rials, American action was not distorted by a compelling economic interest such as oil. None of these conditions exists in Iraq – because both the politico-economic circumstances of the country and the mind-set of the occupying forces are so different: as Dower remarks, 'the United States is not in the business of nation-building any more'. In fact the Japanese analogy cruelly highlights what was so unpropitious about the American occupation of Iraq. If heeded before the war, the 'lesson' of 1945 might have alerted the Americans to the very bleak prospects for an early disengagement from the country.[18]

The Japan–Iraq analogy is an example of how illuminating it can be to reflect on the difference between two ostensibly similar situations. But if the variable and contingent nature of historical change is kept in mind, it follows that the most insight will be gained from exploring a range of analogies which bear on the present in different ways. Within the Johnson administration in 1965 only two precedents counted for anything: Munich and Korea, both of them interpreted as supporting military action. Very little account was taken of Dien Bien Phu, the disastrous defeat suffered by the French in 1954. This precedent not only raised the possibility of defeat in a land war; it also highlighted the nationalist and anti-colonial dimension of the conflict. Had the administration kept an open mind while it subjected each of these analogies to rigorous testing, it might have acquired greater insight into the situation in Vietnam. Instead George Ball, the one official who took up the Dien Bien Phu precedent, was outgunned by his colleagues.[19] When critical decisions are required, historical precedents are valuable not because they offer a short cut to certainty, but because they help to keep policy-makers open to a more realistic range of outcomes.

Precedent in English local government

Compared with international relations, the role of historical analogy in domestic policy is less emotional and less controversial – and for this reason has attracted far less attention. Domestic policy is not immune from morally laden analogies. For fifty years the Slump of the 1930s retained its analogical power as the ultimate cautionary lesson, reaching a climax during the depression of the Thatcher years in the 1980s, when unemployment once more became an acute social problem. But domestic policy does not exert the same dramatic pull as foreign policy, nor is it populated to the same degree by larger-than-life villains and heroes. For these reasons the popular grasp of domestic history is weaker, and people are less likely to apply historical analogies to current issues in welfare or education. In this less fevered atmosphere, analogical thinking can yield rich dividends.

One instance is the debate among historians addressing the issue of what needs to be done to revitalise local government in England. They have examined two earlier periods with this question in mind: first, the 1870s and 1880s, when modern municipal government took shape; and secondly, the 1930s, when elected councils made some of the most innovative responses to the Slump in London and elsewhere. The mid-Victorian period was when the modern idea of accountable and technocratic municipal authorities came into being. Birmingham under Joseph Chamberlain aimed to transform the lives of its citizens by intervening decisively in social welfare and public health. Other cities soon followed. In order to achieve these goals, they were prepared to challenge the shibboleths of the day, notably by extending public ownership of utilities: 'gas-and-water socialism' as it was disparagingly called. Simon Szreter has identified the preconditions of the great age of enlightened municipalism. First, there was a culture of civic pride and service to the community, initially urged by the Non-Conformist churches, and then taken up by business leaders like Chamberlain. Secondly, there was a buoyant electoral base, recently expanded by the Second Reform Act in 1867. Thirdly, municipal councils enjoyed financial autonomy, which allowed them to raise rates and take out loans to finance ambitious schemes of improvement. This autonomy was important because it enabled cities to build up programmes finely attuned to local particularities (which in turn stimulated local politics), rather than apply a one-size-fits-all model from Whitehall.[20]

By no means all late Victorian councils were paragons of enlightenment. But in the best of them, Szreter claims, New Labour 'will find an extraordinary treasure-chest of parallels and analogies to inspire them'.[21] Now, as then, the fundamental requirement is to unlock the energies and resourcefulness of local communities. Low turn-out in local elections is profoundly indicative of a malaise of commitment, and needs to be addressed. Local government also needs to be able to call once more on the services of the ablest and most public-spirited. For that to happen, local government must have the freedom to develop policies suited to local circumstances, and it must have much greater financial autonomy vis-à-vis central government. In 1870 local government expenditure was 32 per cent of all government expenditure (rising to an all-time record of 51 per cent in 1905); by 1999 the proportion had sunk to 24 per cent as a result of the 'capping' of local rates and limitations on council borrowing.[22]

In effect, Szreter is singling out the most innovative period in the history of English local government and asking what can be learned from it today. The persuasiveness of this analogy depends on how well the two contrasted conjunctures are contextualised. Can the guiding principles of the 'civic gospel' be implemented once more, or have the enabling conditions which made it possible disappeared during the intervening century or so? When Szreter says that history gives a resounding 'yes' to the question of whether British society today has the resources to improve itself, the answer can only partly depend on a reading of the mid-Victorian achievement. It requires two further lines of analysis. First, how long the distinctive characteristics of nineteenth-century urban government survived: a restricted franchise, a relatively homogeneous electorate, and a culture of deference had all disappeared by the end of the twentieth century, as Tristram Hunt has pointed out.[23] Secondly, some grasp is needed of the political forces which emasculated local government in the 1980s, and whether they are still in existence. Szreter says little about the context in which New Labour operates.[24] If, for example, the public now values equality of provision between different authorities above municipal independence, a reforming agenda derived from the nineteenth century may be doomed.[25]

In another History & Policy paper Jerry White also draws lessons for local government from the past, but he is able to shed light on the context of present-day decision-making, partly because he uses a much shorter time-scale. His starting point is a comparison between London's local government now and in the 1930s, during the heyday of Herbert Morrison ('Mr London'). Between them, the

LCC and the borough councils controlled hospitals and health services, emergency services, poverty relief, education, and electricity production – much more than what their successors control today. White pinpoints two periods in which local control of services was dismantled. One of these was (unsurprisingly) Margaret Thatcher's time in office, when privatisation drained away many of the powers of local councils to special-interest bodies, like housing associations and school governing bodies, which had only a very partial accountability to the wider community. The other period was the creation of the Welfare State in the immediate postwar years. The new services brought in by the Attlee government were managed from the top. Aneurin Bevan pushed through the centralisation of the NHS, including the voluntary hospitals, in the teeth of opposition from local interests and their champions in the Cabinet. That centralist approach to social services has remained influential in the Labour Party ever since. New Labour speaks with two voices, on the one hand introducing executive mayors, but on the other, intensifying the switch to special-purpose bodies, for example in Foundation Hospitals. White makes the telling point that, far from being a novel and progressive solution, these institutions hark back to the plethora of special-purpose bodies (for sewers, public libraries, etc.) which the reform of Victorian local government was designed to streamline and democratise. The 'New Localism', as Labour calls these initiatives, is only the latest element in what has become a very substantial democratic deficit. The practical inference to be drawn from White's work is that centralism is a Labour vice as well as a Tory one, and that this needs to be kept in mind when interpreting present-day Labour statements about the Welfare State.[26]

Both Szreter and White are politically engaged, in the sense that they have strong views about what local government today could and should be like. But their analogies are carefully controlled. They do not suppose that history will repeat itself. Szreter, in particular, brings out how the 'civic gospel' of Chamberlain's Birmingham was just that – a Christian imperative of service, which could never be replicated as part of a revived municipalism today. Each writer is concerned to rescue from present-day pragmatism certain principles of governance that were expressed through specific forms in both the 1870s and the 1930s, and could (in their estimation) be made the basis for further innovation today. There is an element of prescription here, but it is not one which forecloses other options: if anything, there is a morbid sense of what the other alternatives are all too likely to be. The purpose of the analogy is to exhume from oblivion a tradition of English local government which might guide us to a more effective system in the future.

Crises of masculinity: then and now

The directness of the analogies that Szreter and White draw is refreshing, but their angle on the past is perhaps less innovative than it seems. Ever since the Webbs wrote their studies of English local government, it has been clear how modern practice has continued to draw on old models. Indeed, because policy-making means taking decisions, it is not unusual to be guided by the past, even if that past is a distorting mirror. Analogical thinking is less often acknowledged in thinking about social behaviour and cultural attitudes. But it can nevertheless illuminate aspects of modern experience, particularly those which are assumed to be without precedent.

Gender relations provide an interesting example. Today's sensibilities about relations between the sexes seem to inhabit a completely different world from fifty years ago. The difficulties that many men experience in the new climate of greater gender equality are commonly summed up as a 'crisis of masculinity'. The phrase itself is new, and it describes a phenomenon which is also taken to be new. 'Crisis' seems the appropriate word to refer to disorienting changes which are affecting men at the same time in quite different spheres. First, men are said to be losing the battle of the sexes. Women have won advancement at the expense of men in the workplace and in public life, and much anxiety is now focused on the extent to which boys' performance in school is slipping behind that of girls. The balance of power has also shifted within the family: divorce proceedings are more often than not initiated by wives, and child custody is awarded to the mother in the majority of cases. Secondly, the labour needs of the economy are changing to the disadvantage of men. There is less and less demand for the unskilled physical strength of young male school-leavers, while in the professions men can no longer expect their working life to be shaped by the unilinear career in which so much of middle-class masculine identity has been invested in the past. 'If work used to define masculinity', writes Anthony Clare, 'it does not do so any more'.[27] Thirdly, masculinity has been re-defined by profound changes in sexuality. Gay liberation was the catalyst for opening up a strictly heterosexual male culture to a kaleidoscopic diversity of styles and practices: heady liberation for some, but profoundly disorienting for those whose chief aim is to 'fit in'. Then there is the AIDS epidemic, at its height a threat to all who were sexually active, but a threat in particular to the time-honoured equation of masculine prestige with sexual 'scoring'. This tale of woe might be summed up by saying that men are not only losing power and influence, but have forfeited their legitimacy as the dominant sex.[28]

To a remarkable extent, the gender troubles of the 1990s were presaged by those of the 1890s. Indeed, in 1990 Elaine Showalter wrote a popular text on the *fin de siècle*, *Sexual Anarchy*, with precisely this premise. During the 1890s the masculinity of the middle and upper classes was brought into question on two fronts. First, by what the media of the day called the New Woman, or in a rather more precise catch-phrase – 'the revolt of the daughters': that is, educated young women of the middle class who renounced the protection of home in order to lead independent working lives as journalists or teachers. They lived alone or with a woman friend; they mixed freely without a chaperon – a social trend perfectly symbolised by the woman cyclist; and they claimed intellectual equality with men.[29] Secondly, although the 'New Woman' label was applied only to unmarried women, changes in the status of wives were equally far-reaching. The married woman of the 1890s was the beneficiary of a series of legal reforms over the previous twenty years which had enhanced her rights of property, her rights of child custody, and her right to seek redress against marital assault. Many observers believed that apart from their legal significance, these changes gave wives a new dignity and confidence, prompting them to seek a separation in some cases.[30] At just the time when young men were having to negotiate with women on more equal terms, the rights of husbands over their wives were becoming conditional. It was a widely held view that patriarchy would never be the same again.

How did men react? Leaving aside a small group of progressive pro-feminists like Edward Carpenter, the dominant reaction during the 1880s and 1890s was to reaffirm sexual difference – to define masculinity in terms which made the least possible concession to the feminine.[31] Manliness was given a sharper, more aggressive edge. Physical courage and stoic endurance became the exemplary masculine virtues, ruthlessly imposed on the young, especially in schools. They were seen to best advantage in the lives of military men like General Gordon or Lord Kitchener, who not only never married but kept women at arm's length. But this was more than a pulling up of the drawbridge in the sex war. Fear of women in the social arena was closely associated with fear of the feminine within. The door was shut on emotional disclosure for men by the new cult of the 'stiff upper lip'. Above all, the man who engaged in same-sex practices was defined as 'the homosexual', degenerate and effeminate – indeed degenerate *because* he was effeminate. That image became firmly lodged in popular consciousness as a result of the trials of Oscar Wilde in 1895. And because homosexuality was pathologised in this way, it was obsessively detected – on the streets of the metropolis, in the public schools, and in high places. If any doubt was entertained about the devastating consequences of vice, the authority of Edward Gibbon could be invoked: in *The Decline and Fall of the Roman Empire* (1776–88) he had famously attributed the decline of Rome to the moral canker at its centre. The British Empire was seen by some to stand in no less a peril.[32]

The parallels between the 1890s and today are obvious: the general assertion of women's rights, the rise in female employment, the shifting balance within marriage, and the cultural disorientation arising from ambiguous sexualities are immediately recognisable. Even AIDS was foreshadowed by the highly publicised scourge of syphilis. The fact that these disparate trends coincided during the same decade and caused considerable anxiety among men of varied backgrounds is enough to establish that today's crisis of masculinity is by no means the first. But the differences are important too. The extent and nature of the male response today is very different. As the principal threat to manhood, the New Woman was only a distant relative of her modern-day sister. The aspiration to gender equality was there, but the scale of women's advances now dwarfs anything achieved in the 1890s: most of all in employment, especially the employment of married women, but also in education, in marriage and in parenting.

There was even less similarity in the sexual climate. We live in an era of sexual permissiveness which is truly without precedent. In the 1890s high culture reflected a preoccupation with deviant sexualities, but the numbers of men who were in a position to benefit from a less conventional sexuality were minuscule; and those who engaged in physical relations of any kind with other men were open to the serious criminal charge of 'gross indecency' – the catch-all under which most sexual offenders were prosecuted after 1885. There is simply no comparison with the visible and accessible gay culture we have known since the 1970s, or with the real sense of choice that men now have in defining their sexual orientation. Lastly, commentators today speak glibly of a male backlash, but it is restrained compared with men's reactions at the end of the nineteenth century. The backlash today extends to campaigns to restore the custody rights of fathers and to reverse the scholastic lead of girls over boys. The *fin de siècle*, on the other hand, was marked by a separatist masculinity which disparaged and postponed marriage, and which stigmatised deviant males as 'degenerate'. In fact the present time is more remarkable for the extent of change and adaptation on the part of men. The phrase 'new men' was only occasionally used in the 1890s, but today it is rightly taken to indicate a significant shift in masculinity. Men in the 1890s faced different challenges and responded to them in a distinctive manner.

It is facile, then, to suppose that the gender crisis of the 1890s was re-played during the 1990s. But that does not render the analogy void. Pointing up the differences over time is a useful exercise in a culture which is still inclined to locate men and masculinity outside history: witness the essentialism implicit in the adage, 'boys will be boys'. Many people today believe that the constituents of masculinity are 'natural', and that what has happened in recent years is not a modification of masculinity, but its dismantling. The focus on the 1890s shows that even a hundred years ago the conventions of manhood were understood differently, with the implication that masculinity is not cast in stone. If masculinity has changed since the 1890s, it can change again, without necessarily signalling a total collapse. In that sense it makes a difference to know that today's men do not face an unprecedented crisis, and that an earlier generation experienced a comparable sense of disorientation.

* * * * * * *

Most high-profile historical analogies – like the persistent recourse to Munich – are unreliable because of the unequivocal guidance they purport to give. They assume a near-identity between 'then' and 'now'. They deal in single causes and moral absolutes, and they are usually paraded as the *only* historical argument with a bearing on the present situation. The case against this kind of analogy can be summed up by condemning it as a form of presentism: it is asserted most vigorously by people intent on validating or discrediting specific options in the present. The implication of these arguments is that historical analogy not only tells us little; it may actually stand in the way of other, more valid insights.

If the balance-sheet were completely negative, historians would have no reason to concern themselves with analogy. But fastidious withdrawal is not a responsible option, and for two reasons. First, in thinking about the past, as in other areas, analogy is one of the basic reflexes of the human mind. No amount of refutation will reduce its role as a means of getting to grips with the unfamiliar. The task for historians is to define the ways in which historical analogy can be used so as to promote real understanding of the present. This brings me to the second point. The genuine benefits of analogy are not as dramatic as popular usage sometimes suggests, but they are by no means inconsiderable. They depend not on a presumed convergence between past and present, but on the demonstration of difference alongside similarity. Correctly applied, analogy enlarges our sense of possibilities rather than narrowing them down to a single prescription. Finally, analogies must be considered alongside the other modes of historical understanding which have been discussed in earlier chapters. Our readiness to see repetition between past and present must always be qualified by a presumption of difference. Most important of all, whatever point in time is under examination – whether past or present – it must be understood sequentially. In the case of Vietnam, the value of analogical thinking would have been greatly increased if it had not excluded attention to the history of Vietnam itself.

In this situation historians have two public tasks. First, analogies that are based on bad history and merely provide specious support for a particular policy need to be exposed for what they are, before they do too much damage. But secondly, analogies which serve to refine understanding of the present are a genuine asset to critical debate, and historians should be less reticent about articulating them in public. Measuring English local government against the practices of the past has achieved some publicity.[33] On the other hand, public awareness of the relevant historical perspectives on current issues of gender is very poorly developed. Analogical thinking is too prevalent for historians to ignore, and too mixed in its outcomes for them to reject it out of hand. It is a dimension of historical awareness which cries out for more discriminating demonstration.

5

The Family 'in Crisis': a Case-Study

Up to this point the application of history to public understanding has been illustrated by means of a rapid succession of briefly ana-lysed issues, in order to demonstrate that historical perspective is an asset across the entire spectrum of public debate. But it is not easy to register all the implications of applied historical thinking from this rapid *tour d'horizon*. In this chapter the threads of the argument are brought together in relation to a single theme, in order to demonstrate the different levels at which historical under-standing can bear upon a complex issue. The family has been an object of social and moral concern in Britain since the 1970s. Dur-ing the 1980s under Margaret Thatcher it rose to the top tier of the political agenda, spawning intense public debate. The attention of historians was attracted to this field because official policy rested on assumptions about the history of the family which were manifestly mistaken. But academic scholarship offered more than this. Current research on the history of the family not only served to expose the political appropriation of the past; it also offered historical perspec-tives which made for a much more accurate reading of the present state of the family – and one which was considerably less negative than the picture presented by the political Right.

The politics of family crisis

The 1980s were the last moment in British political history when the government of the day made a confident appropriation of the past to support important areas of policy. During the run-up to the 1983 election Margaret Thatcher demanded that there should be a return to 'Victorian values'. At the time it seemed an almost quixotic appeal, given that 'Victorian' had so recently been a by-word for social neglect and aesthetic ugliness. Thatcher re-defined the Victorian era as the period when British business had made the country great, when the state had kept its distance from people's lives, and when the family had been the bedrock of morality. Each of these elements was intended to resonate with popular concerns, but perhaps none more so than the last. During the 1980s there was extensive press comment about a rising divorce rate, single mothers, and disorderly youth. The family, it seemed, was 'in crisis'. Such a diagnosis was at root historical, since it rested on a pessimistic contrast between 'then' and 'now'. The discourse of 'Victorian values' was therefore highly appropriate to this end.

The family in crisis was one of the most distinctive contributions of the Tories to political discourse of the 1980s and early 1990s. It was first adumbrated by Keith Joseph while the party was in opposition during the 1970s. By 1979 the Conservative Party was claiming to be the party of the family, in contrast to the supposed permissiveness and collectivism of Labour. Margaret Thatcher developed this strain with increasing confidence during her premiership. As she remarked in her most famous aphorism, 'there is no such thing as society, there are only individuals and their families'.[1] John Major was, if anything, more emphatic about the need to support family values – it was a prominent plank of his ill-fated 'Back to Basics' campaign. The rhetoric of family crisis did not entirely disappear with the departure of the Tories in 1997. In his first speech to the Labour Party Conference as Prime Minister, Tony Blair pledged that every policy and initiative would be tested 'to see how we can strengthen families'. Compared with the Tories, however, Labour has been much more cautious about exploiting popular anxieties about family life, and much less drawn to historical contrasts. It is not simplifying matters too much to treat 'the family in crisis' as a Tory idea, and to analyse it with reference to the years from 1979 to 1997.

The crisis was presented in essentially moral terms. Divorce and juvenile delinquency were the tell-tale evidence of a generation in thrall to short-term gratification. And whereas this hedonistic tendency had in the past been held in check by social discipline, the law now condoned immoral behaviour: Labour had during the 1960s enacted 'permissive' measures on divorce, abortion and homosexuality – a record which gave a hard political edge to the Tory rhetoric on the family. The state had further undermined the family, by distributing welfare payments which not only assisted genuine casualties, but rewarded individuals for irresponsible behaviour. This too could be blamed on the Labour Party. The representative target of these concerns was the lone mother, who stood for the moral irresponsibility of the 'liberated' young, the collapse of parental control, and the bottomless pit of benefits on demand. The nation would prosper if the family were strengthened; and individuals would flourish and grow if the family was the first charge on their moral and social obligations. Mrs Thatcher claimed that previous governments had neglected these basic truths, and the result was a crisis not only in the family, but in the fabric of society: 'the basic ties of family', she emphasised, were 'the very nursery of civic virtue'.[2] Her government set out to address the crisis by straight-talking on the virtues of traditional family life, and by pruning the welfare system.

A diagnosis which attributed so much to 'the Sixties' was bound to make great play with what went before. The traditional family was treated as both a reproach to the present generation, and an aspiration. Tory rhetoric depicted it in morally one-dimensional colours. Spouses honoured their vows and stuck together through thick and thin. The home was a bastion of male authority, where due deference was paid by wife and children to the bread-winning *paterfamilias*. The old were nursed and cherished until their dying day. Most important of all, the family was where the character of the upcoming generation was formed, through a balance of training, discipline and affection. A measure of its success was an absence of hooliganism. And all this in an atmosphere of privacy in which human relations could be cultivated without outside interference.

Any notion of crisis in the family is premised on a sobering contrast between the instability of the family now and the supposed stability of the family at some time in the past. That time is usually unspecified, often expressed as timeless tradition. And so it might have remained if Thatcher had not been drawn to reflect on her Victorian heritage during a TV interview in April 1983. A few weeks later she made explicit the link between Victorian values and family life, describing her own upbringing in these terms:

> You were taught to work jolly hard, you were taught to improve yourself, you were taught self-reliance, you were taught to live within your income, you were taught that cleanliness is next to godliness. You were taught self-respect, you were taught always to give a hand to your neighbour, you were taught tremendous pride in your country, you were taught to be a good member of your community. All of these things are Victorian values.[3]

For Thatcher, the Victorian period was exemplary in two respects. On the one hand, rates of economic growth that in the 1980s could only be dreamed of were achieved by untrammelled entrepreneurship, with the added bonus that personal wealth thus accumulated had been invested in the social fabric through large-scale charitable giving. On the other hand, the family had provided the foundation of a stable society, in which parents took responsibility for their own, and self-reliance and self-respect were inculcated in children, along with a sense of duty towards community and country. In subordinating their personal gratification to the good of the household, family members had been trained to be useful members of society. Here Mrs Thatcher was describing her own recollected childhood in the 1930s, but by attributing her upbringing to her grandmother she was able to lay claim to a Victorian formation. In the same breath she called the principles of her upbringing 'perennial values', which implied that authority for good practice could just as well have been drawn from earlier periods. The reason for the Victorian focus was that it enabled Thatcher to make the connection between domestic virtue and economic success. In this she echoed a characteristic strain of Victorian teaching – 'Happy homes are among the chief causes of a prosperous country', wrote one didactic author in 1881.[4] The rhetoric of Victorian values implied a neat convergence between individual morality and economic rationality.

It is not easy to disentangle the sentimental and the philosophical from the politically down-to-earth in Thatcher's thinking. At a pragmatic level, talk of family crisis, by shifting attention to the responsibility of the individual, was a useful diversionary tactic from rapidly mounting unemployment (the jobless total was running at 3 million by the time of the election in May 1983). 'Victorian values' also provided powerful reinforcement for a key objective of the government – to reduce the charge made by families on the welfare state, and thus fund sweeping tax cuts. The Tories characterised the family as an essentially autonomous institution, which had been undermined by a culture of dependency and by the constant meddling of welfare professionals. For Thatcher, this state of affairs confirmed the validity of a more profound truth: that the family was the strongest bulwark against the extension of state power into the lives of its citizens. She is said to have been much influenced by a book along these lines called *The Subversive Family* (1982), by her policy advisor Ferdinand Mount.[5]

At a rhetorical level, Thatcher wanted to talk up the standing of the Conservatives as the 'pro-family' party, identified with those traditional values that older voters yearned to see restored. Thatcher's language – especially her recollection of discipline and purpose in childhood – was music to the ears of such people, without committing her to anything. Attacks on permissiveness had a comparable generational appeal. In a society experiencing many transformations within the span of a single lifetime, most people require an area of life which stands for continuity and security. The family is widely taken to fulfil that function, offering the promise that the most intimate aspects of experience can be kept separate from the maelstrom of change. Yet the family is unavoidably implicated in social change. The very forces which drive society towards new forms of economy, technology and culture exact their toll on family relations. The deep levels of anxiety about the family which periodically surface in popular culture arise from the fact that the family appears to be failing in its fundamental functions. As Jane Lewis has remarked, 'The family is regarded as bedrock and yet it is also feared to be fragile'.[6] As a result, the need to locate the ideal family in the past is hard to resist. The sense of loss is intensified by the feeling that what is vanishing in the present had 'always' existed heretofore: its disappearance now, if not final, is a massive reproach to the moral fibre of today's generation. For the very old, the context may be a rosy-tinted image of early childhood; for younger people the ideal family is located beyond their direct experience – before the Sixties, before the war, or 'in olden times'. But the actual period chosen is immaterial, for the ideal manifestly belongs to traditional time rather than historical time. It expresses an authentically conservative view, not only because it is tailor-made for certain policies of the Right, but also because it expresses a heavy pessimism about the condition of mankind.[7]

The Victorian family: actual and imagined

The past that Margaret Thatcher's policies were ostensibly committed to re-creating was located in the Victorian era, extended to include the 'Edwardian summer'. Notwithstanding the efforts of historical revisionists, the period before 1914 is still widely regarded as an innocent world of social stability and untroubled patriotism, when the pace of life was on a human scale. The popular image of the Victorian family so familiar from memoirs and photographs is of a piece with this appealing picture. It appears to be the linear ancestor of our own most valued conventions of domesticity: comfort and fireside pursuits; hierarchy and respect; reciprocity between the generations; and a judicious balance between discipline and affection. The cast of characters features a nurturing angel-wife, a man of business refreshed and restored by the wholesome atmosphere of home, well-behaved but happy children, and cherished grandparents. The bourgeois provenance of this model is unmistakable. But it was not so very different from the 'traditional' working-class family discovered by sociologists in the 1950s, dating back to the late nineteenth century, with its carefully maintained privacy, independent bread-winner, house-proud wife, and a quiverful of children properly educated for the first time in the new Board elementary schools. The correspondence is close enough for the working class to share some of the supposed credit of the bourgeoisie as exemplars of 'family values'.[8]

The correspondence of this 'Victorian' model with social reality was limited. In the 1860s the bourgeoisie scarcely numbered more than 100,000 households. The lower middle class of clerks and shopkeepers, among whom bourgeois verities were most prized, comprised approximately one million households. There were a further million working-class families which enjoyed a 'family wage', good housing and a reasonable margin above subsistence. In fact, the 'Victorian' model applied to 30 per cent of the Victorians at most.[9] The proportion rose significantly during the late nineteenth century, but half the population was left untouched. The remaining 70 per cent led very different lives. Low wages meant that most if not all family members had to contribute to the income of the household, and even their participation might not be enough to prevent occasional application for relief from the Poor Law authorities. In areas like Lancashire and the Potteries, up to 30 per cent of married women worked outside the home at the beginning of the twentieth century. Over the country as a whole, the proportion of married women at work had by the same period fallen to 10 per cent. But this figure did not include taking in work at home. Much of this out-work fell on children. Child labour in factories was almost a thing of the past by this period, but informal and unregistered child labour was rife. It proved largely impervious to the introduction of compulsory education until the school-leaving age was pushed up to fourteen in most parts of the country, by 1914. With all family members required to earn some kind of wage, the 'rough working-class' domestic economy has been aptly termed one of 'forced interdependence'; no more striking contradiction of the supposed complementarity of the Victorian family could be imagined.[10]

The standards of health and privacy prescribed by sanitary experts were modest enough, but they were confounded on a large scale by overcrowding in multi-occupied dwellings: in 1901 there were over 100,000 such 'homes' in London alone.[11] We know from the frequency of the registration of births soon after the marriage of the parents that sex before marriage was commonplace; it was a traditional feature of betrothal. When bad faith or adverse circumstances frustrated this expectation, the result was a 4 per cent illegitimacy rate and a rising number of abortions. Ten or even a dozen pregnancies were not uncommon, with perhaps six surviving children in the middle class, and somewhat fewer in the working class. Domestic violence existed at all levels of society, but it was particularly prevalent in the homes of the rough working class. Most commonly blamed on drink, 'wife-beating' reflected the insupportable tensions of surviving on the edge of penury, and the humiliation of male unemployment in particular. Children were at risk also. Between 1889 and 1903 the NSPCC intervened on behalf of a total of 754,732 children, for reasons of neglect, violent assault or 'moral danger'.[12]

Retrospective golden ages are invariably selective: it is asking too much of them to encapsulate an entire cross-section of social experience. But the 'golden age' model of the Victorian family is open to the further objection that, even when applied to the top 30 per cent to whom it strictly refers, it seriously distorts historical reality. Integral to the bourgeois family were a number of negative features that few people would wish to revive today. In fact, ever since the post-Victorians made their angry protest after the First World War, there has been a negative counter-image of the Victorian and Edwardian family which emphasises its patriarchal oppression, its dependence on exploited labour, its pathology of sexual denial, and its stifling boredom. Most historians stand somewhere between these two extremes – exposing the tensions which arose from the rigorously complementary gender roles within the household, while allowing for some degree of sexual compatibility.[13]

Those carefully posed photographs of prosperous family groups disguise the endemic insecurity of Victorian family life. The insecurity was of two kinds. It was material in that the economic supports were unreliable: unemployment or insolvency were frequent and often came out of the blue, and there was little protection against either. More distressing and just as unpredictable was the threat to life: 12 per cent of children born in 1861 died between the ages of 5 and 25.[14] Those that survived faced the real possibility of parental death: 22 per cent of children aged 10 in 1861 had lost one parent.[15] The elaborate rituals of Victorian family life held meaning at various levels; but in part they can be seen as an affirmation of endurance over the material and physical perils of life.[16]

Women paid a high price for the apparent stability of the classic 'Victorian' family. Unless death or sickness intervened, a wife faced an entire lifetime of ministering to the needs of others. Given the size of families, mothering her own children might occupy twenty or thirty years of her life, followed by meeting the needs of her own and her husband's parents. From this career of care there was little escape. To remain unmarried was regarded as failure; it was also usually a penurious existence, as only very gradually did the list of approved occupations for a respectable spinster extend to work of professional status. Middle-class wives were not supposed to work at all, or at least not for payment: philanthropy was the only completely commendable activity outside the home, partly because it was understood as an extension of the familial ethic of self-effacing service. Working-class women were not subject to the same restraining convention, but they suffered from severely unequal pay. Allowed by law in 1878 to seek separation from an abusive or neglectful husband, many wives were deterred from doing so by the impossibility of supporting themselves and their children. The 'angel mother' ideal rested on a structure of coercion and discrimination.

The sexual side of marriage is less open to generalisation, but there is no doubt that the odds were heavily stacked against female enjoyment of the marriage bed. Young women were lucky if they learned even the most basic facts of life from their mothers, and they were unlikely to find other sources of enlightenment. Their spouses, on the other hand, were permitted – even encouraged – to notch up sexual experience before marriage. The scale of prostitution in Victorian England was considered a public scandal, but attempts to control it were directed at the prostitutes rather than their clients. Women who strayed from the road of propriety were harshly judged by the double standard of sexual conduct. Denied sex education and limited in most cases to a single partner for life, the most that can be said of tens of thousands of women is that they had little idea of what they were missing. The only respect in which women were advantaged was in same-sex relationships. Lesbians were frowned upon, but they were not outlawed, whereas male homosexuals ran the risk of the full weight of the criminal law against sodomy and 'gross indecency'.

Victorian public discourse was discreetly reticent about marital sexuality. What it emphasised instead was a companionate ideal, based not on identity of interest, but on a tightly fitting complementarity. The difficulty here was that complementarity was so often experienced as a yawning chasm, and this was particularly evident in the choice of friends and leisure pursuits. Husbands mixed with other men in clubs and taverns, or on the football ground. Wives inhabited a women-only milieu of neighbours and maternal kin. Husbands and wives shared the common space of home, but in other respects belonged to different spheres. This made the position of the *paterfamilias* particularly unstable. The relatively recent separation of work from home posed the question of how to make one's presence felt in a domestic world which was in all essentials the wife's creation. Hen-pecked passivity would attract social humiliation. Over-assertion, leading to violence against wife and children, was another response which was certainly not confined to the rough working class.[17]

Even the notion that the Victorian family was the nuclear family *par excellence* does not hold water. One-parent families were commonplace, though the usual cause was not divorce but premature death. At the turn of the century, when mortality rates had already been brought down, approximately 25 per cent of children had had experience of being raised by one parent.[18] Nor was the Victorian family nuclear in the sense of excluding non-family members. A family which echoed the modern convention of two parents and two or more children was, in Victorian terms, a social failure. All middle-class households employed live-in servants, two or three being the standard establishment in comfortably-off families. The lower middle class, and even some among the more prosperous artisan class, strained every nerve to afford one domestic, often in cramped accommodation. In Victorian culture, family was equated with the 'natural' ties of blood and matrimony, unsullied by mammon, but a market relationship lay at the heart of it.[19]

Only in its relations with the outside world did the Victorian family conform to the modern reading of the nuclear family. Nuclear composition does not, of course, necessarily indicate social isolation, but the world of Victorian and Edwardian domesticity was essentially private and secluded. Whether in the suburban villa or the terraced house, respectability was marked by the closed front door and heavy drapes. This was a reflection of Victorian anxieties about social standing in a period of great spatial mobility and 'new' money. The Englishman's house became his castle in a fuller sense than ever before. Traditional forms of surveillance by neighbours could no longer be relied upon. Few working-class people would interfere with wife-beating in a neighbour's house.

The Victorian family is therefore very inadequately represented by the myth of fireside domesticity. Women were compelled to endure a level of restriction which would be completely unacceptable to the majority of both sexes today. Free sexual expression was denied to all save heterosexual bachelors. Husbands and fathers were often ill at ease in the feminine atmosphere of the home, and they were typically detached from its emotional cross-currents. Above all, the conventional picture of the Victorian family runs counter to the experience of the majority of the population; yet that experience was a precondition of the middle-class model, delivering an abundance of exploited domestic labour, and supporting a level of social inequality on which bourgeois domestic comforts depended.

The fallacies of Golden Age history

The popular rendition of the Victorian family purports to show not only how family life *should* be conducted, but how it was *actually* conducted, and hence how it might prevail again. Indeed, the Victorian period stands not so much for a specific historical dispensation as for an entire tradition, on which the Victorian material casts a particularly brilliant light. Its rhetorical impact would not be increased by exploring periodisation, or social change, or the specifics of historical context. What matters is the privileged access that the Victorian period appears to give to a traditional family world which has endured without change until the recent past – and which still lies within our power to revive. Not for nothing did Margaret Thatcher call her Victorian values 'eternal'. Programmes of political action then become restorative – concerned not to react to what is new, but to reclaim what is thought to have been the Victorian genius for family life. But the very gap between the imagined happiness of the past and our own fractured world intensifies the sense of failure and the lack of confidence today. Since few people actually believe that the traditional family can be restored, policy initiatives are suffused with a deeply held pessimism: all that can be done is to shore up a crumbling structure and slow down the disintegration that lies ahead. Assumptions of decline breed a defeatism which in turn weakens the capacity for creative action.

Part of the problem with the conservative version of the Victorian past lies in the misreading of evidence. Beliefs about the antiquity of the nuclear family are a case in point. During the 1970s conservatives derived much comfort from the findings of the Cambridge Group for the History of Population and Social Structure that the two-generation or 'stem' family had been the characteristic English form since the Middle Ages. Yet this was hardly confirmation of the traditional status of the nuclear family as understood in modern times. Peter Laslett and his colleagues discovered that the multi-generational household of southern Europe was absent from England (and northern Europe in general). They did not maintain that the typical early modern household was confined to family members. Indeed the reverse was the case. It featured servants, lodgers and apprentices, the first two being still very much in evidence in Victorian times. Furthermore, the atmosphere of privacy and seclusion that has come to be integral to the idea of the nuclear family is even more recent: it was the achievement of the Victorians, and even then had limited purchase outside the urban middle class.[20]

But the errors are more systematic than that. The traditionalists' view of the history of the family is one of unrelieved decline. One of the reasons why academic history made little impression on conservative discourse during the 1980s is that at that stage its most influential practitioners (such as Lawrence Stone) were committed to a modernisation model of gradual improvement in the way people behave towards spouses and children since the seventeenth century.[21] Advocates of the decline thesis, on the other hand, maintain that the evils of family life in our time are *new* evils. Some are indeed new. The scale of sexual promiscuity among teenagers and young adults is hard to imagine without the transformation in sexual behaviour which followed in the wake of the Pill. But in other cases the assumption of novelty is misplaced. For example, the sexual abuse of children, which causes such acute anxiety today, was one of the concerns – along with neglect and violence – of the NSPCC from its founding in 1883. The Incest Act was passed in 1908 because the offence was believed to be so common. Equally, young people who by their antisocial behaviour seem not to have internalised the discipline of the family have been a recurrent concern since the days of the 'riotous apprentice'. The class antagonism implicit in much modern discourse on this subject can be traced back to the popularisation of the term *hooligan* at the end of the nineteenth century.[22]

Perhaps the most blatant misreading of the Victorian past is in the sphere of state welfare. Nowhere has the political need for the 'right' past been more pressing. The solution canvassed in some Conservative circles of 'restoring' families to the dignity of self-sufficiency by cutting off welfare support has in fact never been attempted, because it would have precipitated widespread starvation. The Victorians, so often written off as heartless oppressors of the poor, spent very substantial amounts on Poor Law provision and on private charity directed at indigent families; they channelled far more resources into 'outdoor relief' (i.e., cash payments to claimants) than into the infamous workhouses. The record is particularly striking in the case of old people, a majority of whom received regular payments from the Poor Law authorities for most of the nineteenth century. The idea that families had sole responsibility for looking after 'their' old is a fantasy.[23]

Golden Age rhetoric is also marked by a blithe disregard of historical context. This is one of the dangers in tracing back the history of a very specific area of life with blinkers on. Whatever point in the past is chosen, the family can only be understood as part of an entire social order, embracing economic life, religion and popular culture. When that is done well, not only are apparent resemblances between then and now called into question, but also the very notion of 'the family' as a discrete and uniform area of experience. As invoked by the traditionalists, the family is an abstraction, divorced from the historical contexts which gave it meaning.

Just as the ideal family of the past resists the notion of context, so it fails to take account of major changes over time. It relies on a simple juxtaposition of 'then' and 'now', with no explanation of the contrast – beyond the collapse of moral fibre since the 1960s. So the changing structure of the labour market, which cut back on child labour in the late nineteenth century, and then radically intensified the demand for female labour during the twentieth century, has no place in the traditionalists' account. The very factors which might make it possible to understand why the family is a different institution from what it was a hundred years ago are excluded.

The historian's perspective: difference and context

Faced with a political interpretation of the Victorian family which is seriously distorted, historians rightly attach much importance to setting the record straight. But the correction of error raises the question of what should be put in its place. The answer is not the replacement of one orthodoxy by another. Unlike the Tory view, the findings of historians do not support a single perspective. Here, as in other areas of research, interpretation takes multiple forms, influenced by theoretical orientation. For example, feminist scholarship starts from the premise that the family is a patriarchal institution, deeply oppressive of women; liberal modernisers, on the other hand, take a more benign view of the family as a 'haven from a heartless world'.[24] As a result, alongside some well substantiated findings – particularly in the areas of demography and family structure – academic enquiry generates grounds for intense debate. Translated into political discourse, this produces a relative openness to different perspectives and different prescriptions. At the same time, the diversity of interpretation demands to be judged according to the key criteria of historicity – difference, context and process: the same principles which underpin the work of demolition. These are the procedures which yield the clearest illumination of the present state of the family and the direction it might be taking in the future.

Consider first of all the perspective of historical difference. Traditionalist thinking about the Victorians might be regarded as obsessed with difference – that is, the damning contrast between 'our' laxity and 'their' moral fibre. But understanding of that difference is inhibited by its subordination to a crude polarity: the Victorian family is perceived as an unqualified moral good, the mirror image of the derelict family of today. Yet freed from that prior judgement, the difference of the past enables us to ask genuinely searching questions about our present state. Victorian families which approximated to the traditionalist ideal – the top 30 per cent – had many children, full-time mothers, and fathers who played little or no part in the running of the household. These features prompt a number of questions which bear on family life today: how has the quality of childcare changed, now that parental care is concentrated on one or two offspring? Are spouses whose roles replicate each other more likely to live in harmony than those whose roles are clearly demarcated? What does the engaged father bring to his children that his bourgeois Victorian forebear did not?

Once an effort is made to explain these differences, historical context becomes crucial. It is by identifying the enabling conditions of the day that we can begin to understand both Victorian family life and our own. In the case of the Victorians, three conditions were central. First, without domestic service the Victorian bourgeois model would have been unattainable. The ideal of the 'angel mother', attentive to every changing mood of her children, was predicated on her distance from cleaning, fire-tending and cooking. That servants were so readily available was due to the decline of the rural economy after 1850 and the steady influx of young women into the towns. Those conditions had ceased to obtain by the 1920s, though in the longer term their disappearance was partly made good, first by the arrival of electrical household appliances, and then by an influx of foreign girls seeking domestic work in childcare. The second condition was the monopolisation of the public sphere by men. This not only entailed the near-total exclusion from paid work of middle-class women. It also gave men maximum prestige within the home as sole earners and sole carriers of public burdens. Today, while that division of labour may prevail in many families, the cultural norm which once sustained it has been undermined, and with it the assumption of masculine superiority. The third condition was the sanction of religion. In respectable Victorian families the duties owed by husband and wife to each other and by children to their parents were strongly upheld by Christian teaching. Religious belief may have been on the wane from mid-century onwards, but this indicated no retreat from Christian morality: 'godless Victorians' were noted for their strict personal code. Today by contrast, the churches have far less influence, and their pronouncements on family morality sometimes suggest an accommodation with the secular mores. Manuals of marriage and childcare may adopt a prescriptive tone, but they carry no sanctions.

These vanished conditions of the Victorian period may be set alongside the historical conditions which have formed the contemporary family. Here, the most critical issue is the demand for married women's labour. In pre-industrial households of the middling sort, wives took a share of the professional or artisanal activity on which the family income depended. But since production was located within the home, they seldom went out to work. To the Victorians who feature in the Golden Age model, paid labour for married women could only be understood as a state of poverty in which the wife was compelled to desert her natural duties. Today, the prominent role of married women in the workforce is one of the key determinants of family life, in both poor and comfortably-off households. Without it the value attached to motherhood would not have diminished, and children would probably be subject to more supervision at home. Above all, the phenomenon of the working wife has major implications for the relationship between spouses, pushing it towards forms of equality which were utterly foreign to the respectable Victorian.

Two-income families are consistent with another enabling condition of contemporary family life: the ethos of egalitarian individualism. This is generally attributed to the 'me-generation' of the Sixties and the radical demands of 'second wave' feminism in the ensuing decades. As a result, marriage approximates now to what Anthony Giddens calls a 'democracy of the emotions'. Its rationale is emotional communication; when the channels of communication dry up, there may be little else to sustain the marriage.[25] Even more remarkable from the perspective of the traditionalist, children are to a considerable extent included in this democracy. They are more likely to be consulted with regard to family decisions, and more likely to determine how they spend their time. Entirely consistent with this is the presumption that children should not be subject to corporal punishment by their parents.

Finally, the contemporary family is profoundly conditioned by its economic role as consumer. Rising incomes have expanded the scope of consumption, and TV advertising creates the desire for additional needs. But these needs are not confined to the family in a collective sense. Every member is a consumer, and his or her wants – as parent, toddler, teenager and so on – are the subject of specialist production and niche advertising. Critics may deplore the materialism of contemporary family life, both in itself and because it is a weak foundation for family cohesion, but consumption now provides the principal economic rationale for the family. The perspective that sits best with the findings of historical research regards the Victorian era not as a reproach to us to strive harder for 'standards' in family life, but as a benchmark of how our society has been transformed – and with it the actual conditions in which family life is conducted.

The historian's perspective: process and innovation

The juxtaposition of 'then' and 'now' is not, therefore, bound to lead to a nostalgic mind-set. Applied in an open-minded way it can bring into focus what is distinctive about our condition, and lead to some grasp of what has made that distinctiveness possible. But for the full significance of the difference between 'then' and 'now' to be understood, the enabling conditions must be seen, not just as snapshots in time, but as the outcome of process. One of the reasons why two-income households and the egalitarian ethos of marriage have become such marked features of family life is that they are the outcome of trends that have developed over several generations. They have become integral to our society and culture through an extended process over time.

The wife earning wages on her own account – as distinct from working in partnership with her husband – was an innovation of the Industrial Revolution. Much criticised in its day as a denial of woman's nature, it was a feature of the Lancashire cotton mills throughout the nineteenth century. But it was less prevalent in other sectors of the economy, and during the latter part of the century the percentage of working wives actually declined. A start–stop pattern also characterised the twentieth century. Substantial expansion of women's employment during the two world wars was partially reversed when peace returned. But since the 1950s the trend has been continuously upward, suggesting that the increasing proportion of married women at work is part of the logic of capitalist development.[26] What is at issue is a fundamental structural feature of the family, which will surely continue – and may intensify – in the future.

Nor was the ethos of equality within marriage conjured out of nothing in the late twentieth century. An egalitarian code of personal relations was implicit in the tenets of classical liberalism, as reflected in the writings of John Stuart Mill, for example. In the late nineteenth century the status of middle-class married women began to be enhanced by legislative changes to their property rights, and by the advocacy of feminist campaigners. When Beatrice Webb described her marriage to Sydney Webb as 'our partnership' she was tapping into a familiar convention among intellectuals and professional people. In the 1950s, critical discussion by family experts focused on companionate marriage and 'teamwork' – a relationship between complementary equals rather than a hierarchical institution. By that time the rising proportion of wives who contributed to the household income gave a material basis to the claim to equality. By contrast, the 1960s and 1970s marked a genuine new departure with regard to children's rights. Public campaigns for children in families had focused on dire poverty and extremes of cruelty; they had not championed the rights of the generality of children to be heard as well as seen.[27]

A comparable perspective can be brought to bear on the identification of the family with consumerism. Although highly characteristic of our age, it is not new, but rather a reflection of the longstanding tendency of British manufacturers to cultivate the home market in preference to overseas markets. That process was already discernible in the late nineteenth century and has been a growing feature of the economy ever since. Mass advertising took off in the same period, and during the inter-war years women's magazines fulfilled a similar role to that of television now in fuelling consumer demand. Here, as in regard to working wives, our sense of the possible needs to be informed by a sense of the trajectories in which we find ourselves.

In one field it makes sense to jettison the language of process and to recognise revolutionary change, and that is contraceptive technology. Of course there is an earlier history of contraception, but before the 1960s the impact of the condom, the cap and the pessary was held back by a combination of cost, discomfort, unreliability and social stigma. The Pill changed all that, first for wives, then for unmarried women. Small families had mostly been achieved by abstinence; now they were compatible with a sexually fulfilling marriage. As for single people, the fear of pregnancy has historically been the most powerful deterrent to extramarital sexual activity. In the course of about ten years it effectively disappeared. To urge chastity on young people today is to ask of them self-control unsupported by any other consideration (except the fear of AIDS for a few panic-stricken years in the mid- to late 1980s). That is a situation without precedent. The indirect impact of the Pill is also significant. Mothers can not only limit their child-bearing, but can time it to suit the demands of a career, thus further enhancing their job prospects. And since the consequence of effective contraception is usually to reduce the total number of births, married women typically look forward to several active decades after the last child leaves home. This too is a novel development, with important consequences for divorce and for women's employment. Effective forms of contraception mean that there is no possibility of putting the clock back on these changes.[28]

Such instances of revolutionary novelty are rare. More typically, historians play the opposite role, disputing the assumed novelty of current practice. This approach is particularly effective when applied to the prevailing political discourse of the family 'in crisis'. The 1980s were not the first time the alarm has been raised. The Victorians and Edwardians themselves experienced two 'crises', marked by anguished diagnoses and draconian solutions. In the 1840s social observers were appalled by the inversion of gender roles in the households of female factory workers, and by the stunted growth of children in the industrial towns, especially where they were employed in those same factories. During the first decade of the twentieth century, in the aftermath of the Boer War, anxieties about national defence and military fitness led to renewed scrutiny of the working-class family, with mothers cast as the villains of the piece. Again, as recently as the years immediately after the Second World War, the family was seen to be threatened by a low birth-rate and rampant divorce; poor mothering was singled out, particularly for its contribution to juvenile delinquency. All these episodes of introspection shared a morbid preoccupation with the small percentage of families having acute problems, to the exclusion of the well-functioning majority.[29]

Yet in each case the severity of the crisis was talked up for reasons which had as much to do with economic or political anxieties as with the state of the family. The nineteenth-century bourgeoisie – the very people who benefited most from the new capitalist order – lived by a family ethic which elevated intimacy, nurture and leisure, in contradiction to the freedom of the market and the atomisation of the individual. Working-class people strove to live by the same ethic, but the main function of their families was to reproduce the labour requirements of capitalism. Tomorrow's workforce would only materialise if minimal standards of health and child socialization were practised today. Capitalist expansion encroaches on the family, and yet at the same time depends on it for its future prospects. Karl Marx was fully alive to that tension, predicting the demise of the family in industrial society. From the perspective of earlier crises, the recent agonising about the family's prospects reflects not an unprecedented catastrophe, but a recurring symptom of contradiction in the social fabric. To the extent that family life *was* in crisis in these earlier periods, the durability of the family would seem to be indicated, and with it, all the more reason to moderate our fear of change in the present.

* * * * * * *

Since the 1980s anxiety about the state of the British family has been marked by stories of gymslip mums, non-providing fathers, and young people beyond parental control. New statistics on the soaring divorce rate and on welfare support have stoked the concern. This material may look like an unmediated reaction to today's news. But behind the headlines lies a historical proposition – that the nuclear family is in the process of collapse. 'Victorian values' provided vivid shorthand for this belief and enabled the Conservatives to strike a chord with some sectors of public opinion.

One of the marks of a mature democracy is that such claims are put to the test of critical appraisal. Historians have the appropriate expertise. At one level, their role is to refine the definition of the nuclear family in the light of past experience, to enquire how prevalent it was (even in its heyday), and to consider whether it was an unqualified blessing. A further stage is to identify the varied range of factors – demographic, economic and ideological – which transformed family life during the twentieth century. Not all of the traditionalists' picture falls victim to this appraisal. They are correct, for example, in assuming a greater degree of parental supervision and a lower level of promiscuity among young people during the Victorian era. Where they are wrong is in generalising from these features a golden age of family values which were lived as well as preached. Wrong too is the representation of the massive changes that have occurred in the structure and tone of family life as a fall from grace for which our generation carries the principal responsibility. Recognising as much frees us from the past as moral reproach. Energy can instead be redirected to identifying solutions to new problems – not in a prescriptive way but in the spirit of opening up current debate to alternative perceptions of the family in the past and the present. As the distinguished historian of family John Gillis has put it: 'if history has a lesson for us, it is that no one family form has ever been able to satisfy the human needs for love, comfort and security'.[30] The history of the family merits study because it uncovers the huge variety of family-living in the past, thereby disclosing some of the possibilities which are available in the present. It protects us from the most constraining illusion of all – that there is only one way of managing our social arrangements.

6

History Goes Public

The argument of this book so far assumes that historians have at their disposal the means to reach beyond their academic peers and their students. This proposition must now be put to the test. And since the weight of academic tradition has seriously questioned whether dissemination is desirable or feasible, it is clear that searching questions must be asked. A gulf is usually said to exist between the academy and popular history, and for good reasons. The questions which interest the academic historian and a general lay readership often seem like oil and water. The language of the monograph is poles apart from that of the TV spin-off or the coffee-table book; and there is a sharp divergence as regards the rigour with which facts are established and arguments sustained.

The many faces of public history

Today, however, the distinction is not so sharp. There exist the makings of an alternative practice dedicated to crossing the gulf: public history. While still marginal to the academic profession, public history is taking an increasingly prominent profile, as measured by conferences, outreach activities and publications. But the term 'public history' needs to be used with care. Its scope is still uncertain. Ludmilla Jordanova has defined it to include all the means by which those who are not professional historians acquire their sense of the past, but, as she concedes, this is very much an umbrella definition.[1] It conflates highly disparate activities whose only common ground is that they modify the traditional relationship between professional and lay history in some way. Of course, that common factor is highly significant, but it means very different things to the various constituencies who are brought together under the umbrella of public history. In one register, 'public history' refers to everything that professional historians do to bring their work to public attention – through journalism, TV programmes or policy advice. In another register, it refers to historical work carried out in conjunction with museums and other heritage bodies, partly in pursuit of a conservationist agenda, and partly in order to promote the public consumption of the visible and tangible relics of the past.

In yet another register, 'public history' refers to historical work carried out in the community, always out of fascination with the past, and sometimes as an assertion of ownership over the past, through oral history, family history and other community projects. Here the role of the professional historian is one of support and advice, working alongside amateurs, often on their terms. History Workshop during its heyday in the 1970s and 1980s was a notable instance of this convergence between amateur and professional, bringing together trade unionists, feminists, freelance writers and academics. Indeed, the project of a democratised public history is now sufficiently established for historians to study it as a cultural phenomenon in its own right, most notably in Raphael Samuel's *Theatres of Memory* (1994).[2] Yet, in the last resort, professional historians are peripheral to these endeavours. The initiative generally lies with the community, and scholars assist rather than initiate.

At the other extreme from this community-based activity is history written for corporate bodies and the public authorities. This aspect of historians' outreach has been a marked feature of the USA. There too, public history means different things, but the most robust – and certainly the best funded – kind has been historical work commissioned by government departments and private corporations. Public history began in the mid-1970s in somewhat inauspicious circumstances. American academia was experiencing a jobs crisis as university appointments failed to match the big rise in PhD enrolments. Public history was a means of enhancing the status of trained historians who might have expected an academic career but found themselves working for non-academic employers. As one exponent put it, 'public history is the adaptation and application of the historian's skills and outlook for the benefit of private and public enterprises'.[3] Developing a business culture loomed large in the house journal *The Public Historian*, founded in 1978. By the 1980s most government departments employed historians on a substantial scale. Although the label 'public history' was new, the practice dated back to the New Deal, when archival work was promoted by the Federal Government on a large scale. During the Second World War, 54 government agencies employed professional historians to write an objective record of their activities before it was overlaid by the tumult of events. But in the 1980s the growth area was policy advice. Historians were employed to investigate the circumstances in which a specific policy had originated, and to evaluate a range of policy options.[4]

This vein of public history is also found in Britain, but to a much smaller extent. One of the reasons why British historians tend not to label themselves 'public historians' is that very few are employed in the public sphere; whatever public history they do is only a small part of their professional activities. Major corporations like Unilever and Reuters have employed historians, but their remit is to write company histories rather than to advise on policy. The government also employs historians, but sparingly and only in certain departments. Not surprisingly, the Foreign Office, with its concern for diplomatic precedent, has the most strongly felt need of 'departmental memory'.[5] During the First World War it employed historical advisors. The young Charles Webster was commissioned to write an account of the Congress of Vienna of 1815 as orientation for the 'officials and men of action' who were making peace at Versailles.[6] The Foreign Office set up a full-scale Historical Branch in 1944, which now comprises nine historians. Their principal role is to prepare the official documentary history of British foreign policy. But they also give historical advice to officials when asked, usually in connection with some historical controversy which has entered public debate and is causing embarrassment to ministers: one such case was an alleged cover-up regarding the disposal of 'Nazi gold' in 1996.[7] The Cabinet Office also employs historians. On the other hand, the Department of Health does not, despite the strong element of historical continuity in certain areas of policy such as the management of public health scares.[8] Whether the availability of historical expertise in government departments actually improves the quality of policy-making is open to question. Historians who have penetrated behind the Whitehall façade are not impressed. Zara Steiner concludes, 'No Foreign Ministry has yet found a satisfactory way effectively to bring past memory and record as construed by historians into the policy-making process'.[9]

More to the point is whether government-sponsored history should be regarded as public history at all. Confidential historical advice is not intended to reach the public domain and seldom does so. Published official histories are in a different position, but they may serve as a smoke-screen rather than to enlarge the effectiveness of public scrutiny. On the other hand, such histories may genuinely enlarge the sum total of evidence available to the public. This was certainly true of the multi-volume publication of British documents on the origins of the First World War, which was commissioned from G. P. Gooch by prime minister Ramsay Macdonald in 1924.[10] But the suspicion remains that historians working for government or corporations have their hands tied. Commitment to public enlightenment takes second place to institutional affiliation. It is more faithful to the spirit of the phrase to confine 'public history' to work which is directly addressed to the public.[11] Without a customer or a paymaster, the historian is then placed in the much more challenging position of striving to reach a lay audience.

Each of the models of public history discussed so far has its place in the practice of historians. Governments and corporations should certainly not be denied historical advice on the grounds that the political virtue of the scholar may be impugned. At the other end of the scale, academic historians have a role alongside the amateur and the activist in crafting histories which speak to the community – understood both in its general sense and as an expression of identity politics. Yet neither fully accommodates the core activities of the professional scholar. It is hardly stretching the meaning of the term to assert that 'public history' includes the dissemination of work which, while carried out in the academy, speaks to public concerns. Communicating the findings of professional historians through the written word and the broadcast media is no less 'public history' than the grass-roots investigations of the amateur. Both are means whereby the non-historian acquires knowledge about the past. Of course, the outreach work of academics does not necessarily promote critical debate. Much of it treats history as entertainment: the good story, the alluring ambience, the historical who-done-it. Occasionally (as during the First World War) historians have put their names to outright propaganda. My concern in this chapter is with critical public history, by which I mean historical writing which addresses a general readership with the intention of fuelling public debate: in short, a history for citizens.

The tradition of public history in Britain

What then does it mean, to treat the findings of professional scholars as 'public history'? What is the framework in which historians can disseminate or popularise their findings? How can they define a relationship with the public which is neither didactic nor subservient? These are not new questions, and the varied ways in which they have been answered in the past are suggestive. Before the professionalisation of history in the nineteenth century, historians were expected to address the educated public in terms which resonated with current politics, and they regularly did so – from Clarendon in the seventeenth century to Macaulay in the mid-nineteenth. It is sometimes supposed that the austere disavowal of topicality by Ranke and his followers brought this tradition to an end. In fact, Ranke was far from being the undisputed model, and historians who practised 'history for its own sake' worked alongside others who loudly proclaimed the relevance of their discipline. The widely read Cambridge historian J. R. Seeley maintained that 'history is the school of statesmanship', and he certainly regarded his studies in the history of British colonial expansion in this light.[12]

During the first half of the twentieth century three distinct kinds of public engagement stand out. In a category by himself was G. M. Trevelyan, the most widely read historian of the century. In works like the *History of England* (1926) he aimed to reprise the achievement of his great-uncle, Lord Macaulay, not only in sales but in celebrating the unique political and social development of

Britain, and the unique national virtues which had made this possible: resilience, calmness, and love of liberty. David Cannadine, his biographer, speaks of Trevelyan's achievement as a 'public educator', and Trevelyan conceived this role in the broadest terms.[13] History was a humane education which could illumine the present, but it did not furnish context or perspective for any current preoccupation. What Trevelyan communicated was an increasingly negative stance towards industrialism, urbanisation and democracy. The past became a refuge rather than a means of engaging critically with the contemporary world.[14]

The second strand of what would now be called 'public history' focused on international affairs. British interpretations of events in continental Europe between the wars were heavily influenced by the issue of war guilt. If Germany was to blame for the First World War, the Treaty of Versailles appeared a just settlement. If Germany's responsibility was no greater than anyone else's, it followed that Germany had been treated too harshly and was justified in contesting the treaty. Historical interpretation was at the heart of this controversy. G. P. Gooch led the pro-German camp; R. W. Seton-Watson maintained a more critical position towards the Central Powers. That British opinion swung during the 1930s to an anti-Versailles position was in some measure due to the intervention of historians like Gooch.[15]

The third strand of public engagement focused on social and economic questions. It was strongly associated with the Left and with one historian in particular – R. H. Tawney. Tawney undertook a number of commissions from the government, but it was his lay readership that mattered most to him and which made his reputation. He wrote both 'relevant' history and works of social criticism which drew on historical perspective. Tawney believed that economic history – unlike political history – spoke to the lives of ordinary people, like the working men to whom he had taught the subject early in his career. His most influential publication was *Religion and the Rise of Capitalism* (1926). Christian economic thought before and during the English Reformation might seem an unlikely theme for a book with such a wide readership, but it was an effective position from which to promote a critical debate about the detachment of social ethics from the conduct of business in modern capitalism. Whatever the rights or wrongs of church involvement in economic questions in the modern world, Tawney demonstrated that it was manifestly false to dismiss it as a modern innovation. In the same way, Tawney bolstered his discourse on equality with a cogent historical account of how the characteristic forms of present-day inequality had come about.[16]

Trevelyan, Gooch and Tawney wrote as individuals, and they would have bridled at the suggestion that they 'spoke for history'. But they did work against a background of professional support for 'relevant' history. The Historical Association was founded in 1906 partly in order to counter the lack of historical perspective in national and imperial matters. A. F. Pollard, the first editor of its journal *History*, aimed 'to bring the light of history to bear in the study of politics ... to test modern experiment by historical experience'.[17] That objective continued to be met between the wars, when the Association was in the thick of public debates about foreign policy and the League of Nations. In the second half of the century the profession ceased to identify with any public function outside the educational system. The Historical Association was no longer concerned with the 'usable' past; as Keith Robbins has remarked, its journal 'sounded a more severely "professional" note'.[18]

The main exception to this postwar retreat from relevance was the Marxist historians, whose influence was greatest between the 1960s and 1980s. They produced one public historian of commanding stature. E. P. Thompson dominated the lay readership of social history even more than Tawney had done in the 1930s. Like Tawney, his ability to connect with a wide audience was grounded in his experience of teaching in adult extension classes: how otherwise could he have had the confidence to address a 900-page account of the English working class to the labour movement and working people? In *The Making of the English Working Class* (1963), Thompson was manifestly partisan and quick to make morally loaded judgements. He identified with the exploited and applauded the courage of the activist. But if the book falls into the category of identity history, it was not a triumphalist narrative. Rather, it took the form of a sequence of essays which reflected on both the human realities of industrialisation and the diverse cultures of those who raised their voices in protest.

Professional historians in the public sphere

At the beginning of the twenty-first century nobody dominates public history in the way that Trevelyan, Tawney and Thompson once
did. Yet the number of historians who from time to time work to a
public agenda is much larger, and they can choose between a wider
range of media, including television (see Chapter 7). Their work
affords ample illustration of the main purposes that a critical public
history can serve. From the perspective of the academic historian,
the least controversial of these is the disposing of myth. It places a
premium on their distinctive critical armoury, and it can be applied
impartially to the distortions of Left and Right. 'I should like to be
the counterpart of the eye-surgeon', says Theodore Zeldin, 'special-
ising in removing cataracts'.[19] William Wilberforce's single-handed
achievement in bringing to an end the Atlantic slave trade would
be one such myth – matched by the countervailing belief that the
trade was brought to an end by slave resistance. Britain's role in the
Second World War also provides ample illustrative material. Dunkirk
stands not only for the ingenuity of the British people in retreating in
order to triumph in the future, but for the perfidy of their allies, the
French and Belgians. The truth was that all three countries had been
soundly defeated by the Germans. The popular version of Dunkirk is
grist to the mill of the more xenophobic aspects of Euroscepticism.[20]

As the previous chapter demonstrated, historical myths also prevail in the field of social policy. Margaret Thatcher's espousal of
'Victorian values' gave historians an important corrective role to
perform. Their public response was prompt and cogent. The *New
Statesman* published a special supplement in which seven historians took issue with her interpretation. The contribution by Leonore
Davidoff and Catherine Hall dealt crisply with the hidden oppres-
sions of the nineteenth-century bourgeois family (four years before
they published their major work on this theme[21]). James Walvin
acted as consultant to a Granada TV series on Victorian values and
published a spin-off book.[22] A little later *History Today* carried a
series of articles on specific Victorian themes. Most impressive of
all, Michael Anderson brought to bear his immense demographic
knowledge of the nineteenth-century family, writing effective critiques in the *Guardian* and *New Society*. His piece in *New Society* asked

'What lessons in understanding our own society can the Victorian family offer us?' His analysis was couched in terms of a cautionary tale: to wish to live in Victorian times was 'a dangerous illusion'. The most important lesson from family history, he said, was that 'new institutions and new expectations' need to be developed to cope with new situations.[23] Professions of belief in public history are too often cast in vague terms. Here we can see how the task was undertaken in circumstances which pitched historians against the political wisdom of the day.[24]

Some scholars take the view that the discrediting of myth is the only legitimate public role for the historian.[25] But public history has positive functions also. The role of a keeper of public memory is not only to correct false memories, but to ensure that significant facets of the past are brought into play as and when they speak to present-day concerns. This is particularly true of painful or disturbing episodes which have previously been forgotten or suppressed. The rejoinder 'Why weren't we told?' captures the recognition that what has come to light shifts the moral landscape. That question forms the title of a book by the historian Henry Reynolds about settler–Aborigine relations in Australia, in which he documents the draconian policies pursued towards Australia's indigenous population.[26] Similar reactions have greeted revelations about the history of slavery in the United States.[27] There is much comparable material in Britain's colonial past. The recent publication of two books about counter-insurgency in Kenya during the Mau Mau rebellion – 'Britain's gulag', as one of them calls it – has elicited the reaction that this is a history that people in Britain 'need to know' in order to come to a just conclusion about the process of decolonisation in Africa, and in order to grasp something of the trauma from which many Kikuyu still suffer.[28] In cases such as these, the past appears in a disturbingly alien light, revealing aspects of our own society that we would prefer not to acknowledge. If historians do not recover such material, it is hard to know who will.

Sometimes historians are called upon to bear witness to uncomfortable truths in the formal setting of the courtroom or the public inquiry. This is a mode of public history which has attracted a good deal of attention in recent years. The effect of courtroom procedure is to highlight the validation of facts, at the expense of the web of context and interpretation which may determine their significance. This is likely to reduce the historian to an ancillary role. But in some cases historical facts and the correct use of the research procedures which establish those facts are the very point at issue. Such was the case in the libel case brought by David Irving against Deborah Lipstadt and Penguin Books in 2000. Irving maintained that Lipstadt, in alleging Holocaust denial, had libelled him. Lipstadt's defence was based on the claim that Irving's statements about the Holocaust were false. Since Irving maintained that his views were borne out by archival evidence, the defence was compelled to scrutinise his research procedures. To that end it retained the services of the historian Richard J. Evans. In tracing Irving's statements back to the documents on which they purportedly rested, Evans demonstrated that Irving had repeatedly flouted accepted procedures and mistranslated documents. Evans's findings were central to the judgement in favour of the defence. The case had considerable significance, not only because it placed Irving in a very negative light, but also because it weakened the plausibility of Holocaust denial.[29]

It is rare for a case to turn on one person's research methods in this way. More commonly, historians appear in courts or tribunals where their expertise may have some relevance but where they are unlikely to hold the outcome in their hands. The Saville Tribunal in Northern Ireland is a case in point. The remit of the Tribunal, set up by the British government in 1998, is to determine what happened on Bloody Sunday in Derry on 30 January 1972. The main role of the two historical advisors nominated by the tribunal has been to scrutinise public documents released in breach of the 30-year rule, some of which contain new material. They have had far less to do with the statements of witnesses and the courtroom confrontations. Paul Bew (one of the historical advisors) concludes that the value of retaining historians is that they are more disinterested than the lawyers, and – unlike the public – they know that the findings of the tribunal will still be provisional and flawed.[30] That is a relatively upbeat judgement. Historians' experience of other public forums has been less happy. It has not been unknown for scholars to be hand-picked to support a particular case and to pronounce on questions which in the light of the evidence are unknowable.[31] The Irving case makes the point that for historians, entering the public lists may involve rubbing shoulders with distasteful company. Most academics would prefer to debate with those who know and respect the rules of the game. But given that charlatans and cranks have access to the public ear, it is all the more important that historians expose them for what they are.

In illuminating events like Mau Mau or the Holocaust, historians are of course coming to grips not only with another time, but with another society. Here their educational role is of great importance, given the limited knowledge that the public in Britain (or any other country) has of the rest of the world. Without some grasp of the historical forces which have been at work, foreign societies remain just that: foreign. Popular media comment on other countries rests on two assumptions: the first is that their actions ought to be a 'rational' response to the present; and if they are judged otherwise, this is taken to be confirmation of the second assumption, that 'they' are fundamentally 'other' and unintelligible. Seeing these societies in historical perspective provides an essential foundation for interpreting the actions of their leaders and the social and cultural forces they represent. During Africa's 'decade of independence' in the 1960s, British Africanists led by Roland Oliver not only trained African research students and assisted the new African universities; they wrote for a lay readership in Britain. *The Short History of Africa*, which Oliver wrote with J. D. Fage for Penguin in 1962, provided essential perspective for the unfocused popular engagement with the continent. It brought into public awareness for the first time the scale of Africa's medieval empires, the full legacy of the slave trade – both European and Islamic – and the foundations of African nationalism.

But history not only provides an analytical window on the present; it also gives a vital insight into the political culture of all societies, but especially those societies which outsiders find hard to comprehend. The key is social memory – the body of beliefs about the past that a community holds in common, which sustains its sense of identity, and which is transmitted by cultural means. The priority attached to cultural solidarity means that the content of social memory reflects a highly selective take on the past. In any social or political conflict, the participants carry conflicting histories in their heads, their precise inflection ranging from the triumphalism associated with past victories, to a sense of grievance born of defeat. Social memory is now the subject of a great deal of historical work. Historians are the people best qualified to understand how the past is refracted into so many cultural variants and why they are often at odds with each other.

The break-up of Yugoslavia brought these issues into focus. The acute tensions dividing Serb from Albanian, or Orthodox Christian from Muslim, were rooted in the traumas of the Second World War, the Austro-Hungarian Empire, and even the 600-year-old conflict with the Ottoman Turks. At one level, historians could shed light on the historical forces which had brought the south Slav lands to their present predicament. The war in Bosnia was widely regarded in Britain as a civil war based on ancient hatreds. In a timely historical account, Noel Malcolm pointed out how this assumption led the West to misjudge the measures for bringing the conflict to an end. In Malcolm's view the dynamic elements were not traditional animosities within Bosnian society, but Serbian interference and Western ignorance: 'paradoxically, the most important reason for studying Bosnia's history is that it enables one to see that the history of Bosnia in itself does not explain the origins of this war'.[32] At another level, the intensity of the strife in Yugoslavia needed to be explained in terms of social memory: the tendency of today's participants to situate their actions in a narrative which extended back to selected events during the Second World War, and even (in the case of many Serbs) to the epic defeat by the Turks at Kosovo Polje in 1389. Without some grasp of this extensive cultural hinterland, the succession wars of Yugoslavia made little sense.

Contemporary history

None of the approaches I have discussed so far implies a limitation of the period to be studied. Many questionable myths relate to the remote past, in which lies a good deal of their authority. Painful sensitivities about the past are not confined to the Second World War. And the most illuminating perspectives on foreign societies are often those which draw on an extended time-scale. Nevertheless, the claim on historians of the recent past – or contemporary history – is particularly strong. 'The day before yesterday' is the black hole of popular consciousness – the period which is too recent to have been studied in school, and yet too remote to be accurately remembered. The time-frame of contemporary history is relative. For the older generation it means anything since the end of the Second World War; for younger people, the twilight zone is more likely to begin with the taking down of the Berlin Wall. Accepted notions of the shape and direction of change during the past generation or so tend to be confused and simplistic, and thus much subject to political manipulation. In this context, historical perspective is all the more valuable. Enquiry into historical topics which bear closely on the present, or which remain unresolved, is the rationale for contemporary history – what Hobsbawm terms 'the history of the present'.[33]

An immense fillip was given to the writing of contemporary history by the dramatic and unpredicted collapse of the Communist bloc between 1989 and 1992. Most observers agreed that the world had been changed in a fundamental way: a page of history had been turned. But the real significance of these events could only be plumbed by a long backward glance – reaching back to 1945 or even earlier; 1989 effected a kind of closure on the postwar era. The benefit of hindsight could be brought to bear on the processes and structures of the previous generation.

In just over ten years, three major attempts at re-evaluation were made. Eric Hobsbawm's was the first. Throughout his long career, Hobsbawm has practised what he calls *haute vulgarisation*, by which he means syntheses which foreground the major integrating themes of history for an intelligent lay audience. These include a sequence of three volumes on the 'long' nineteenth century in Europe (1780–1914), and an economic history of Britain since 1750.[34] By 1989 Hobsbawm was stressing that historians' top priority was to tackle the history of the world since 1945, and since then he has followed his own counsel.[35] *The Age of Extremes* (1994) is a history of the 'short' twentieth century, from the First World War to the collapse of Communism. Hobsbawm delineates the shape of the century in two ways. It was the century of the Russian Revolution, in that the period of its global influence extended over almost the entire century. Communism provided capitalism with the means of saving itself from the Depression, and it made possible the defeat of the Third Reich; 1992 represented the final exit of the Russian Revolution from world history. In another sense, Hobsbawm sees the century as a triptych – two periods of great instability enclosing a Golden Age between 1947 and 1973, when the world experienced unprecedented economic and social advance.

Two more recent accounts shift the emphasis from long-term structures to the play of contingency. In Mark Mazower's view, if 1989–92 witnessed the triumph of democracy in Europe, this was not the fulfilment of an enlightened destiny, but the consequence of 'narrow squeaks and unexpected twists'.[36] Such a past should be a warning against complacency about the future of democratic societies. In *Postwar* (2005), Tony Judt takes a similar view of the play of accident, but he highlights the implications for historical consciousness. The lives of Europeans after 1945 had been fundamentally changed by the dictators and their wars, he says, but they could only be reconciled to this by suppressing much painful wartime experience; 1989 ended 'postwar' and removed the self-censorship of collective memory, making many grievances insistently audible for the first time.[37] As Mazower puts it, 'understanding where we stand today requires not only seeing how the present resembles the past but how it differs from it as well'.[38] Both Judt and Mazower are unimpressed by the prospects for a new equilibrium in Europe; stability is less secure than it seems.

Combating AIDS: public history in a time of panic

The range of examples given in this chapter, spanning international, national and social issues, certainly demonstrates the role that historians can play in deepening public understanding of the world. But none of these books is offered as a practical guide to what should or should not be done. Can historians go further and draw out the policy implications of their insights into the past? And will that have any impact on how policy is actually made or perceived? Before considering why such questions are not at the heart of the current debates about public history, it is worth recalling one instance in recent British history when both were answered in the affirmative.

This was the debate in the mid-1980s about what measures should be taken to counter the AIDS epidemic.

Public alarm was intense. It was stoked up by the much higher incidence of AIDS on the other side of the Atlantic: where America led the way, Britain was sure to follow. By 1986 there was intense paranoia in the media, and what one historian has called a *grande peur* among civil servants and politicians, even though only 610 cases had been recorded by that date.[39] The panic was intensified by the belief that this was uncharted territory. No one could recall a time when there had been a lethal sexually transmitted disease of this magnitude. Medical history suddenly seemed relevant in the most practical way. There was prompt recognition of this in government circles: the Health Secretary, Norman Fowler, got in touch with the Wellcome Institute with an urgent request for any relevant historical expertise.[40] The historian who led the response was Roy Porter, a leading authority on the social history of medicine. But Porter was not content with securing the ear of officials. In a crisis which was driven by public panic, he recognised the importance of reaching a wider audience. Porter threw himself into a campaign of public education. He wrote articles for the weekly press, such as *New Society*. He even wrote a signed editorial for the *British Medical Journal* (*BMJ*).[41]

What was at issue? Public support was mounting for compulsion in the fight against AIDS, by making it a notifiable disease, and the fact that AIDS was seen as primarily a 'gay plague' made this draconian solution more acceptable to the public at large. Others regarded this course as an infringement of civil liberties. Porter and his colleagues demonstrated that compulsion was not only that, but also an ineffective way of stemming the spread of a contagious disease. Porter drew on precedents dating back to the plague in early modern England, but his strongest argument rested on Victorian precedent. In the light of high levels of venereal infection among soldiers and sailors, there had then been a vigorous debate about the respective weight that should be given to public health measures and individual rights. In the 1860s the Contagious Diseases Acts (CD Acts) were intended to curtail the spread of venereal disease by requiring suspected prostitutes in designated districts to be medically inspected, and then detained until they were free of infection. The Acts unleashed major opposition from civil libertarians and feminists, and medical opinion declared that they were unwork-able. They were repealed twenty years later. The implication was that compulsion would be no more effective in the fight against AIDS. Perhaps the British government would anyway have settled on a pol-icy of voluntarism in 1987, but historians played a significant part in preparing public opinion for this outcome.[42]

On the face of it, Porter's citing of the CD Acts looks like a crude and superficial analogy: why should mid-Victorian anxieties have any relevance a hundred years on? What justified the analogy was the degree of historical continuity. In most historical epochs sexually transmitted diseases have been stigmatised, and sufferers have there-fore seldom been prepared to divulge them. In that respect, British society in the 1980s differed little from the 1860s. The precedent of the CD Acts was a telling indicator of what can happen when meas-ures of compulsion are adopted which antagonise the very people whose cooperation is essential for containing the disease. This was hardly a new insight, since the lines of debate between voluntarism and compulsion were already established, but it needed to be clearly and calmly stated at a time of acute public alarm.

The circumstances of this case were highly distinctive. Historical insight is seldom regarded as an urgent practical requirement, and government ministers do not often demand solutions from histor-ians. The popular taste for historical analogy, so often condemned by historians, here proved fruitful. Still more unusual was the pub-lic tone adopted by Roy Porter: 'History says No to the Policeman's Response to AIDS', ran the title of his *BMJ* editorial.[43] Very few his-torians would wish to be as prescriptive as that. But an increasing number are prepared to be explicit about the practical significance of their findings. Where historians have made the most significant contribution is in the field of social policy. This is because so many policies in the social field turn out to be adapted from initiatives in the past – sometimes the distant past. Pat Thane's *Old Age in English History: Past Experiences, Present Issues* (2000) draws on some 600 years of social history. Several rosy-tinted images of the position of old people in the past bite the dust. Modern social provision is also conditioned by the past – in the British case by the Poor Law, which lasted from the early seventeenth to the mid-twentieth cen-tury. One reason why the level of the state pension in Britain today lags behind that in other European countries is that under the Poor Law aged recipients of relief received only the barest minimum for subsistence. The long time-frame employed by Thane also enables her to demonstrate the striking continuity in many aspects of ageing in British society. Thus old people in the past did not expect, or want, to share the homes of their grown-up offspring; they preferred to maintain their independence for as long as possible; then as now, they often became a charge on the public purse as a result. The historical record also suggests that policy-makers should place only a qualified faith in demographic projections. As recently as the 1930s and 1940s, authoritative projections anticipated a steep fall in the British population over the next generation, and a corresponding rise in the proportion of over-65s to 30 per cent. As Thane points out, a buoyant birth-rate and rising immigration put paid to that forecast, and a similar fate may lie in wait for today's doom-laden predictions.[44]

History and policy

Thane's work is unusual in being structured round today's policy dilemmas. Historians do a great deal of work which has a bearing on policy without being presented as such. Some of it is taken up in government publications, but, as noted earlier, such work is always open to the suspicion of trimming to the official line. A well informed civic discourse is better served by the independent commissioning of publications which present historical research in an accessible policy-related way. A group of historians acting in this way can highlight policy areas of urgent priority; they can also draw attention to the role that applied historical thinking can play in a critical public discourse.

The first venture of this sort in Britain was the *Historical Handbooks* published by Faber between 1986 and 1991. The series featured concise historical accounts of particular policy areas – unemployment, housing, the punishment of offenders, and so on. Most of these books were content to trace the evolution through time of their particular theme and to take note of different approaches to policy revealed by the historical record. The volumes conveyed little sense of how current policy might be informed by these studies. Avner Offer, the driving force behind the series, was well acquainted with the public history movement in the USA and he had hoped for a sharper sense of 'applied history'. In the event, he had considerable difficulty in getting his authors to step outside the 'history as background' mode.[45] For most of them this was all that could be demanded of historical expertise.[46] There was little in the *Handbooks* to strain the conventions of historical detachment.

This caution is less in evidence in the most recent British attempt to bring historical scholarship to bear on issues of public concern. The History & Policy website (www.historyandpolicy.org) was founded in 2003 by Alastair Reid, Simon Szreter and Pat Thane. It is the only ongoing internet resource in Britain to provide historical perspective on a broad range of policy issues. It was planned as an independent academic venture, with the dual intention of influencing the formation of government policies and informing public debate. Since then it has posted over sixty short papers, on topics as various as Foundation hospitals, animal rights, binge drinking, and the Iraq War. The main emphasis is on domestic policy.

It might be expected that a website with this remit would define history in terms of a very shallow time-span. That has been true of contributions on pensions policy and the financing of healthcare, for example. But these are outnumbered by papers which draw on history well beyond the reach of recent recall. Within this longer time-frame the choice of perspective is crucial. The History & Policy papers demonstrate, once again, that the most convincing and illuminating perspectives on the present come from applying the core principles of historicism. They either develop an analysis in terms of historical process, or reason analogically while taking full account of historical difference and historical context. History & Policy makes a particularly significant contribution in qualifying the presumption of novelty. The recent international situation gives historians plenty of scope to make arguments of this kind. The 'war on terror' is generally thought to be waged against a new kind of terrorist, motivated by religious as much as political objectives, and intent on destroying the enemy rather than on persuasion. Christopher Andrew, who has written extensively on the history of the intelligence services, explains how after 9/11 US intelligence assessed the novelty of

Al-Qaeda by measuring it against the secular terrorism they knew well – for example, the IRA. Yet 'holy terror' has a much longer history, dating back to earlier movements in the Middle East, and the religious wars of early modern Europe. Even before 9/11, Andrew was noting 'a *resurgence* of traditional and cult-based terrorism'.[47] The pool of experience available to those conducting the 'war on terror' runs deeper than the intelligence world seems to be aware of. In cases like these, applied history brings out the way in which the origins of salient features of the present are deeply embedded in the past.

Many History & Policy papers make use of analogical reasoning: they juxtapose past and present rather than tracing the intervening process. Some parallels do little more than confirm a well founded analysis of the present. As part of an argument about the health policies of the West towards less developed countries, Sheldon Watts cites the case of British policy towards the containment of cholera in India. In 1868 the Government of India (i.e. the colonial administration) suddenly reversed the quarantining policy which had been their principal – and largely successful – weapon in the fight against cholera. As a result, hundreds of thousands of lives were lost in the ensuing decades. Watts demonstrates that the critical factor in this reversal was the lobbying by business interests involved in the new Suez Canal. The commercial prospects of the Canal – opened in 1869 – depended on the speed and efficiency with which ships passed through on their way to and from India. Quarantining in Egypt would impose costly delays on ships passing through the Canal. But if quarantining was declared to be ineffectual in India, there would be no reason for the Egyptian authorities to apply it either. Watts draws a parallel with the World Trade Organisation's insistence today that less developed countries should permit free trade in cigarettes. His conclusion is that the historical record gives us little grounds for doubting that profit will prevail over health where relations between the West and the developing world are concerned. It is a rhetorical argument, in that it offers vivid illustration of a well-known feature of development policy, rather than revealing a fresh line of analysis.[48]

The yield of analogy is more valuable when it is employed not to close argument, but to open up current policy to possibilities suggested by past experience. Here, something is recovered from the past which might guide us to more rational arrangements in the future, but no claim of exclusive wisdom is being made. In a History & Policy paper on Northern Ireland in 2003, John Bew sought to counter the reductionist polarisation of politics in the province by invoking an earlier Unionist tradition of creative and outward-looking thinking, symbolised by the prominent role played by the Ulster Presbyterians in the 1798 rebellion. Bew was not suggesting that the world of the nineteenth-century Protestant radicals could be re-created today; rather, he intended to make the point that there could be more to Unionism than the embattled sectarian version which was still dominant in 2003. Recent events leading up to the formation of a Northern Ireland power-sharing executive in 2007 cast an intriguing light on that view.[49] It is the comparison of things that are not exactly comparable which enables us to draw creatively on the diversity of the past. This is also the spirit in which Simon Szreter calls to mind the civic gospel of the great cities of late Victorian England, as a means of critiquing the democratic deficit of local government today (as outlined in Chapter 4).[50] Szreter recognises that the context is very different today. Having shown how the morale and effectiveness of Victorian local government were radically improved, he suggests ways in which these objectives might be achieved by policies attuned to twenty-first century circumstances. This is analogy properly tempered by a sense of historical distance.

* * * * * * * *

The common feature of the historical work reviewed in this chapter is that it originated in academia but was placed before a wider audience in the belief that it also addresses topical issues of public concern. As such, it falls under the heading of 'public history'. Outreach work by academics is certainly not the only form of public history. Indeed, common usage usually implies that public history means a working association between academics and community historians; occasionally academics drop out of the frame altogether. The growth in extramural history – in museums, heritage sites and community groups – represents an immensely welcome addition to popular culture. Its innovative quality depends on the active sense of ownership which animates so many enthusiasts, in contrast to the more passive consumption of the past in earlier generations. The very welcome result is that we now have a much more participatory historical culture. Yet a comprehensive public history requires not only the contribution of academics to community projects, but the free access of the public to the findings of historical scholarship. At present, the varied and constantly expanding body of academic knowledge is the least exploited element in public history. How that situation might be rectified is the subject of the final chapter.

The Citizen's Resource

Historical knowledge has been seen to support the proper function-ing of democratic society in a number of different ways. It can be regarded as one of the most effective means by which the idea of the nation is made a reality in the minds of its citizens: as an imagined community, the stories the nation tells about itself define its char-acter and its claim on members. This interpretation is discredited on the general grounds that it smacks of indoctrination, and more specifically because it conflicts with the diversity of approach pre-ferred in a multicultural society. Alternatively, history can be valued as a means of explaining and justifying the combination civic rights and duties which has been handed down from the past: this pro-gramme of citizenship is highly supportive of democratic values, but here too there is a whiff of instrumentalism as the content of history is adjusted to teach specific lessons. Historians feel more comfort-able with a third justification – that history provides a training in the rational evaluation of evidence and argument, on which democratic discourse depends. This is probably the only perspective on which all historians agree. For some it is the central ground of debate. Yet it amounts to no more than claiming for history a special distinction in aptitudes which are found in other disciplines also.

But there is another case to be made for history as a training in citizenship, which is closer to the intrinsic nature of the sub-ject. Historical perspective enhances the citizen's capacity to make informed judgements about the issues of the day, to participate in public discourse, and to make intelligent use of the vote – in short, to exercise his or her active membership of the body politic. Thinking historically – or 'thinking with history' – means employing historical perspective to illuminate current issues. It means identifying what is distinctive about the present, enlarging our awareness of the possibilities inherent in the present, and situating the present in the temporal flows which link it with the past and the future. In fact history is integral to the critical judgements about matters of public concern which people are expected to make in a representative democracy. From this perspective, the real justification for promoting history as an adjunct to citizenship is not ideological, but critical. British schools in the past have treated history as primarily ideological, and there are still elements of that way of thinking in the political demands for a national or multicultural content. Yet the most valuable role of history in schools is to provide students with the rudiments of a historical mode of thought which will make the world around them more intelligible. That task they share with the media, who carry a major responsibility to apply historical perspective to the analysis of news stories.

The changing profile of citizenship in Britain

Citizenship expresses a set of political values – traditionally, loyalty to the nation state and to the ideal and practice of representative democracy. It confers a variety of legal and social rights – ranging, in the British case, from welfare entitlements to trial by jury – and it demands the performance of a range of duties, such as complying with the law and voting in elections. Some of these elements have a very long history, extending back to ancient Greece. In the Renaissance they re-entered political thought in the form of civic republicanism – a code which in England upheld an ethos of political and military service in the landed elite and bolstered their claim to influence in the state. During the Interregnum in the 1640s and 1650s, radicals like the Levellers promoted a much broader definition of citizenship, based on civic equality and extending to a majority of the adult male population. This more radical agenda was again articulated during the era of the French Revolution, whose foundation document was the Declaration of the Rights of Man and

Citizen (1789). During the nineteenth century, successive instalments of parliamentary reform meant that the electoral system began to catch up with the idea of representative democracy. Citizenship lost its subversive edge. In the generation prior to the First World War it became instead an instrument for imposing on the new electorate a proper sense of its duties and obligations. More recently, citizenship has been brought into higher relief by the unsettling changes that many of the liberal democracies have experienced during the past thirty years: in particular, the decline of class solidarities and the rise of multicultural politics. In Britain, where constitutional convention has not traditionally favoured the concept of 'citizen', the effect of these changes has been marked. One of the more positive results has been the concept of the active citizen, meaning someone who contributes to the civic good through participation in public discourse, associational life and charitable service. Over the past hundred years or so, there have been intense – if intermittent – debates over these and other aspects of citizenship. History has frequently been enlisted in the service of these debates, and it plays a central role in current discussions about education for citizenship.

One hundred years ago 'citizenship' was shorthand for the attitudes of deference and patriotism which were thought appropriate to the lower classes. By two stages – in 1867 and 1884 – the franchise had been extended to working-class men, giving them a majority of the electorate. As Robert Lowe is said to have remarked after the Second Reform Act of 1867, 'now we must educate our masters'. When W. E. Forster introduced the Education Bill three years later, he declared, 'on this speedy provision depends . . . the good, the safe working of our constitutional system'.[1] This meant not only teaching basic literacy, but instilling socially responsible values in children who might know nothing of the wider political world, or who might be exposed to a subversive interpretation of it. School reading books spoke of citizens rather than subjects, but it was a passive kind of citizenship, emphasising obedience, discipline and loyalty to Queen and Empire. History held a prominent place in the drive to promote citizenship because it was readily enlisted to convey these abstract qualities in 'real life' situations. Exemplary lives were usually military or naval in character. They featured prominently in the most widely read citizenship manual of the twentieth century – Baden Powell's *Scouting for Boys*, subtitled 'A Handbook for Instruction in Good Citizenship'.[2]

This approach persisted during the 1920s and 1930s, for example in the observance of Empire Day. But politicians and educators increasingly questioned the terms on which citizenship had been equated with patriotism before the war. Citizenship needed to be re-defined to support the pressing agenda of internationalism. The League of Nations Union campaigned vigorously for the downplaying of war and nationalism in the history curriculum in schools.[3] The historian Eileen Power believed that world citizenship would come nearer if history teaching enlarged the sense of group solidarity and demonstrated that 'everyone is a member of two countries, his own and the world'.[4] At the same time, the rise of totalitarianism in Europe intensified anxieties about the survival of democratic political values in Britain. In response, the Association for Education in Citizenship was set up in 1934 by leading Liberals and Fabians, to campaign for the explicit teaching of citizenship. As the threat from the dictators intensified, education to defend democracy was an increasingly compelling idea, but the Association did not succeed in persuading the government to adopt this policy.[5]

For half a century the debate about citizenship languished. It did not move centre stage until the final years of Margaret Thatcher's premiership. In the course of a single year – 1988 – citizenship was lauded by the Tories and then quickly taken up by the other parties. It has remained a political buzz word to this day. What distinguishes the discourse of citizenship today from its early twentieth-century precursor is the emphasis on active participation in society. Mrs Thatcher's vision of citizenship was certainly not passive. She had in mind a model of the citizen as the willing volunteer, ready to leap into the breach left by retreating state provision in the social services. Through their voluntary and public-spirited efforts, citizens would render assistance where it was most needed, while emancipating themselves from the dead hand of the state. This was social rather than political citizenship. It was soon overtaken by events. New Labour won a handsome victory in the 1997 elections, but on a turn-out of only 71 per cent, which sank even lower in 2001. The political education of an apathetic electorate now rose to the top of the citizenship agenda. In the nineteenth century, citizenship had been seen as a means of preventing people from voting unwisely or subversively; now the worry was that they would not vote at all. Bernard Crick, a political scientist and longstanding advocate of political education, was appointed to chair a committee to advise on the introduction of citizenship in schools.[6] A Citizenship Order was issued in 2000, laying out a curriculum for 11- to 16-year-olds. Schools began teaching the subject in 2002.

History's role in citizenship education

The introduction of citizenship into the school curriculum expressed an important point about the preconditions of effective citizenship. Political theory is primarily about the values which must underpin a participant democracy; historians show how those values have developed from earlier traditions of civic engagement. Yet citizens are ineffectual unless equipped with certain resources of knowledge – about the political order within which their rights and duties are exercised, and about the substance of politics, embracing both domestic and international issues. Crick's programme of citizenship drew on the perspectives of a number of disciplines. Since one of his goals was to produce citizens able to make informed decisions about politics and society, there would appear to have been a high premium on historical understanding. Crick himself believed that 'of all the other subjects History may have (should have) the greatest role to play'.[7] In this regard, his views were not reflected in the provision of citizenship education. In fact, the curriculum introduced in 2002 made little use of history except in relation to the European Union, the Commonwealth, and the issue of cultural diversity.[8] Recently the growing debate about 'Britishness' has led to a greater emphasis on history. Reporting on 'Diversity and Citizenship' to the Department for Education and Skills in January 2007, Sir Keith Ajegbo recommended that British identity be 'studied through the lens of history', and the government signalled its intention to comply.[9] But so far, history teachers have not been given a prominent role in the delivery of citizenship, despite the vigorous case made by history teachers themselves: 'the past', said one group of teachers, 'is the springboard from which citizens learn to think and act'.[10] The teaching of citizenship was either distributed among the existing subjects of the National Curriculum or given to teachers of Personal, Social and Health Education. But that sidelining is beside the point. The reason that history teachers are not more involved in the citizenship curriculum is that their own subject is still regarded as a course in citizenship in all but name. That had been the dominant view of history in schools before the First World War, and it was reaffirmed as recently as 1991 by those responsible for drawing up the National Curriculum in History. The History Working Group, set up to advise the minister on the new curriculum, took the view that their task was to devise a programme which would enable pupils to act as 'informed citizens of the twenty-first century'. They added that respect for people of other cultures, an informed curiosity about the wider world, and an understanding of rights and liberties, must all be 'firmly grounded in history'.[11]

Once the History Advisory Group got down to the detail, the central issue in the proposed curriculum was what balance should be struck between the nation, the world, and the community. The debate was heavily overlaid by ideological considerations. Kenneth Baker, the responsible minister, declared that the curriculum should reflect 'the spread of Britain's influence for good throughout the world'.[12] The Group received a great deal of unsolicited advice. The Right wanted a strong narrative of constitutional progress and national triumph. The Left wanted a curriculum which was both wider and narrower than this – wider in taking on themes from world history, and narrower in attending to the history of Britain's ethnic minorities (thus reflecting concerns about the relationship between citizenship and membership of an ethnic minority). Defining the school curriculum turned into an acrimonious debate about what should be included or omitted, usually on the terrain of identity politics. The outcome was an ungainly compromise which tried to accommodate as many interest groups as possible. The pupil in British schools experiences a bewildering sequence of short units of study – 'the sushi-bar of history'. The shortcomings of this approach are widely recognised, yet even today the debate about pedagogic procedure quickly gets caught up in identity politics. Thus the think-tank Civitas, in urging the restoration of a master-narrative in school history, could think of no better contribution than to offer to every primary school in the land a copy of a children's history written in the heyday of imperialism – H. E. Marshall's *Our Island Story*.[13]

History in the National Curriculum

As currently constituted, the National Curriculum in history aims to touch as many political bases as can be accommodated within nine years of study. For example, pupils aged 11 to 14 are required to take six modules – three British, two world and one European. In political circles the history curriculum is evaluated in an entirely instrumental way, and it is measured against a notion of fully comprehensive coverage. Yet in reality, much of the knowledge of history which pupils acquire in school will prove no more durable than their knowledge of information technology or biology. It will rapidly become obsolete. Equally, no amount of forethought in curriculum design will ensure that students are equipped with the history that is relevant for the major issues of their political lives. Thus no educator in the 1980s could have predicted that Iraq would become such a crucial issue, and it would be unreasonable to reproach the schools for having omitted it from the curriculum.

But covering all bases is not only unrealistic; it also detracts from other kinds of learning which may prove more enduring and more adaptable. History's claim to enhance students' understanding of the world needs to be defined with some care. If the claim rests on the acquisition of knowledge which is specific and topical, then history will always be found wanting, through neglecting many topics which demand attention, and through failing to anticipate the issues that students will face in the future. The case should be argued along different lines. What history teaching can do is to pass on to students the intellectual tools they need in order to interpret the changing world around them. These tools are not primarily the generic skills of argument and analysis that many historians regard as their discipline's main claim to relevance. The vital tools are those that only history can teach. These are the ability to apply historical perspective and to know what are the historically literate questions to ask of any topical issue which calls for understanding in depth. Thus, in the case of Iraq, the 'informed citizen' would not be someone who had studied the history of that country at school, but someone whose historical education had led to the realisation that history is an indispensable basis for understanding an unfamiliar society. The most valuable objective of history teaching is to enable young people to situate themselves in time, to recognise the centrality of change and development in accounting for the world around them, to grasp the merits – and the drawbacks – of historical comparison, and to draw on the past for a richer sense of possibilities in the future. Such an abstract summary might suggest a shift to a much more theoretical approach to the teaching of history. In fact, enough empirical research has been carried out to demonstrate that school students do not need lessons in theory to develop their grasp of historical thinking; they acquire it through the experience of studying the past in a structured way.[14]

This is far from being an original approach. As long ago as 1972, the Schools History Project sought to reinvigorate the teaching of history by getting pupils to think about history as a form of knowledge, characterised by certain kinds of evidence and certain procedures of evaluation. But this approach worked better on the narrow ground of source criticism than on the broader terrain of historical explanation. The Project became heavily associated with 'skills' at the expense of conceptual and social approaches.[15] The same issues were reprised during the debate about the National Curriculum. Here too there was a concern with history as a discipline, alongside the emphasis on content. But in practice this has meant analysing evidence rather than reflecting on the relationship between past and present. The subdivision of the curriculum into free-standing units of study means that the pupils' historical knowledge consists only of fragments, with scant awareness of how they join up in a temporal sequence. The sense of historical distance between 'then' and 'now' remains out of reach, as does the ability to distinguish cumulative process through time.[16] These insights – the essentials of historicism – are the principal casualties of the 'sushi-bar of history'.

Several changes are needed in the history curriculum if schools are to give pupils their best preparation for citizenship. Enough attention must be paid to a fairly distant time in the past, to convey the fundamental difference between past and present, and to introduce the idea of the past as a storehouse of strange but potentially useful experience: ancient and medieval history lend themselves well to this requirement. There must be a chronological framework extending over several centuries, since on that hinges the idea of process and development. It is often assumed by conservatives that such a narrative will be the story of the nation state. But that is only because of the weight of tradition and of a certain kind of politics. The central thread of such a narrative might be built around the evolution of British society from its earliest economies to the post-industrial age, or the evolution of Europe through conflict, conquest and cooperation. What cannot be dispensed with is some means of showing that different episodes fit together as parts of a sequence. Finally, a substantial proportion of school time needs to be devoted to history post-1945. Ignorance of the immediate antecedents of today's problems leads to seriously skewed judgements. A fair proportion of these are based on the drawing of unsound analogies of the kind described in Chapter 4. Contemporary history is the ideal teaching context in which to consider under what conditions historical analogy might be productive. Such a programme would provide a more valuable long-term preparation for citizenship than the current offering. As the educationalist Denis Shemilt has put it, 'if we are true to the values of History per se, we cannot answer for the views that adolescents will express about the contemporary social and political agenda, but we may nonetheless expect such views to be more rational and informed than would otherwise be the case'.[17]

The civic role of history amounts to much more than support for cultural identities and respect for other cultures. It gives people the rudiments of a mode of thinking which enables them to deepen their understanding of the issues on which, as citizens, they will be called upon to take a view. The most important role that history in schools can perform is to instil a mode of thinking which can be applied and adapted without limit. Academics bridle at talk of 'transferable skills' because within the public discourse of education they refer only to forms of training which are generic and rigorously functionalist, like communication skills or information technology. Given the fact that 'transferable skills' are now central to educational discourse, a more effective tactic would be to assert that individual disciplines teach 'skills' whose value lies precisely in the fact that they are *not* generic, while still being relevant and useful. In short, the contribution of historical education needs to be defended, not in terms of this or that discrete body of knowledge, but as training in a mode of thought of practical relevance to citizens. At present this is a perspective which is all too rarely communicated to students studying history at university. Since most of them move into careers outside history, it seems particularly important for them to have a view about their discipline's potential contribution to public debate. A first step would be for them to evaluate the arguments for and against 'relevance', and to consider what application – if any – the syllabus they have actually studied has.

Critiquing nationhood and securing civil liberties

What kinds of insight can historically literate citizens expect to find in the market-place of ideas? Still the most prominent are under-standings of the historical basis of nationhood. But what academic historians now offer under this heading is very different from even thirty years ago. As a result of membership of the European Union, devolution in Scotland and Wales, and large-scale immigration from the New Commonwealth, Britishness has ceased to be taken for granted. It has become a problematic category, from which an appeal to the historical record is increasingly made. An early indication was the appearance in 1989 of a three-volume edited collection on patri-otism, which proved to be much the most successful of the History Workshop series.[18] The real turning point occurred in 1992 with the publication of Linda Colley's *Britons: Forging the Nation, 1707–1837*. Great Britain, she reminded her readers, only came into existence in 1707, with the union between England and Scotland. The growth of a British identity over the next century or so was due to a common Protestant culture, a militant anti-Catholicism stoked by recurrent wars with France, and a shared pride in – and profit from – the expanding colonial empire. The fact that none of these factors can any longer be regarded as a defining attribute of 'Britishness' puts paid to the notion of a timeless national essence; it illustrates the fundamentally constructed character of the nation.[19] Provided they are not too recondite, books which pursue this line of analysis – and there have been several – are sure of extensive media attention.[20] It is a position which both undermines the rigidities of nationalism and promotes a flexible realism in contemplating the changes unfolding in the present.

In parallel with this critical focus on the nation has been the discourse of multiculturalism. Here the role of critical history is to critique the separatism and triumphalism which characterise some popular renditions of community history.[21] Books of this kind are less concerned to raise the consciousness of this or that community, than to demonstrate the antecedents of our multicultural society in earlier relations of trade and conquest. Work of this kind has come to be known as 'postcolonial' on the grounds that it steps outside the colonial mentality which constrained most previous work about Britain and its empire.[22] No historian has achieved more in this regard than James Walvin – though his work began well before the postcolonial came into vogue. Out of a large number of books, *Passage to Britain* (1984) stands out for the directness with which it addressed popular thinking on race. Walvin emphasised the continuing presence of Britain's imperial past, arguing that racist attitudes which were now visited on ethnic minorities at home had once been directed towards the colonised peoples overseas: the Empire had in a sense been 'brought home.' In order to explain that current British attitudes to race were not necessarily set in stone, Walvin pointed out how British perceptions of black people had changed between the 1780s, the 1830s and the late nineteenth century.[23] In 1984 such ideas were much less widely accepted than they are today. At the time of writing, the bicentenary of Britain's abolition of the slave trade in 1807 is prompting a number of distorted readings driven by the exigencies of cultural politics. This is a situation which calls for soundly based historical work for a popular readership, both black and white.

Historians have also addressed an even older tradition of citizenship – the raising of consciousness about the rights and liberties handed down from the past and now in danger of suppression or erosion. A historical treatment often makes for a clearer grasp of why these rights are necessary, how they were secured (often through political struggle), and why they should not be lightly surrendered. All these issues were addressed by E. P. Thompson in his impassioned defence of trial by jury during the 1970s. Thompson maintained that the jury system was being undermined by its removal from certain categories of case, and by the behind-doors vetting of juries. In his estimation these changes amounted to an erosion of faith in the capacity of the ordinary citizen to fulfil a judicial function: 'the jury box is where the people come into the court'. Thompson drew historical parallels with court practice during the much more unstable period of the early nineteenth century to make the case that nothing in present circumstances warranted the assault on the democratic composition of the jury.[24] Since 9/11 the pace of encroachment on the liberties of the subject – or human rights, as they are now termed – has speeded up. Historians are best placed to counter the proposition that today's civil liberties were 'made for another age' and are therefore redundant. They can remind us that previous politicians have faced dramatic changes in the nature of security threats – like the growth of anarchist terrorism at the end of the nineteenth century – and yet have preserved a respect for civil liberties.[25]

History in the broadcast media

Up to this point, the public historian has been portrayed as a writer of books and articles, more or less adjusted for a wider audience. In Britain – unlike Australia and the USA – no study has yet been carried out into the public impact of historical writing.[26] But there can be little doubt that the printed word has long given place to radio and television as the main channel of historical information reaching the general public. Debates on historically critical topics are unlikely to be heard if they confine themselves to the familiar world of print. The opportunities – and constraints – of broadcasting must be brought into play.

Radio has an underestimated record in this respect. As with other intellectual disciplines, the focus on the spoken word without the distraction of images is conducive to analysis and argument. Probably the most successful attempt to realise this potential was made in the USA by the American Historical Association sixty years ago. Beginning in 1937, *The Story Behind the Headlines* was put out weekly, first by CBS and then by NBC. Academic historians were asked at short notice to provide material illuminating a specific headline.

Domestic and foreign topics featured in the series, with foreign ones dominating during the Second World War. The aim was to assist citizens to live 'intelligently as a part of a very complex society'. This was taken to mean an emphasis not on historical facts, but on 'historical-mindedness'.[27] Lasting ten years, *The Story Behind the Headlines* was a distinguished venture in public history, combining topicality and scholarly rigour.[28]

Nothing like that has ever been broadcast in Britain. But the postwar period up to the 1970s saw a great deal of creative commissioning of historical material, partly because historians like Peter Laslett and Daniel Snowman were employed as producers by the Third Programme. Isaiah Berlin and E. H. Carr gave talks in which they were required to avoid too many abstract nouns and too much use of the passive mood.[29] Other speakers offered historical perspectives on the Prague Spring and on Allende's Chile. Peter Laslett himself gave talks which conveyed the excitement of the contrasts he was beginning to analyse between twentieth-century society and 'the world we have lost'. Major historical surveys were attempted on Radio 4 – notably *The Long March of Everyman* which covered British history from the Romans to the twentieth century and extended over 26 episodes in 1971–2. This was also the period in which the Reith Lectures were a major date in the cultural calendar. Several series were notable instances of applied historical perspective – Margery Perham offered a balance-sheet of colonial rule in Africa during the 'decade of independence', mixing personal experience with shrewd political analysis. Still more topical was Geoffrey Hosking's later series of Reith Lectures on the Soviet Union under Gorbachev. Hosking showed how the expanding civil society made possible by *perestroika* was drawing on the legacy of the *mir* (the peasant community) and the soviets during their revolutionary phase in 1905 and 1917. Delivered on Radio 4, these lectures reached a considerably bigger audience than the concert-interval talks on Radio 3, and they were much discussed in the media.[30]

Today the formal lecture has almost disappeared from radio, damned as beyond the reach of the three-minute attention span. It has been superseded by programmes featuring a presenter and a succession of interviewees. History has a prominent place in this new format, and what it has lost in sustained argument it has gained in giving voice to conflicting interpretations. The largest category of history programmes is those which bring to life a vivid moment in the past, or which follow up arresting historical parallels – as in Jonathan Friedland's series *The Long View*. But radio can also deliver critical historical reappraisals which bear more directly on the present. The Radio 4 series *The Things We Forgot to Remember*, presented by Michael Portillo, aims to close the gap between popular and academic renditions of the past, and to challenge the way highly selective recall becomes entrenched in public memory. Its programme on the 1945 Labour government showed that the Welfare State was far from being the exclusive achievement of Attlee and his ministers; it drew on extensive bipartisan planning during the war, and the Conservative Party was already committed to many of the measures implemented under Labour. The consensual aspects of the Welfare State place the more recent political controversies on this topic in an interesting light.[31]

But it is on television that the prospects for a widely disseminated public history chiefly depend. For most people in Britain, TV is almost certainly the prime source of historical knowledge. In one sense they are well served: history has never been given so much airtime as today. But academics have been vociferous in their criticisms. History on TV is seen as intensifying a tendency for the public to be familiar with only twentieth-century history, and maybe only the two world wars, because archive film and the recorded interview are the sources most suited to the medium. Yet it is evident from the recent success of Simon Schama's *History of Britain* and David Starkey's programmes on the Tudors that television has overcome these technical limitations and is well able to represent remote periods of history on the screen. A more serious criticism is that history documentaries settle on an interpretation in advance, and then select the visual evidence to fit; in this way the controversies that surround many topics of TV history are barely hinted at.[32] But this is to misunderstand the nature of the medium. A narrative composed of a sequence of visual images has many virtues, but it cannot represent argument and counter-argument; it is almost bound to convey a confident certainty. On the other hand, that narrative certainty usually reflects the personal view of a highly visible presenter: increasingly, documentaries are built round a high-profile

personality, foregrounding his or her 'take' on the subject-matter
to the exclusion of other perspectives. No one watching the final
episode of Schama's *A History of Britain* could have imagined that
his reflections on the twentieth century through 'The Two Win-
stons' (Winston Churchill and 'Winston Smith' of Orwell's *1984*)
were anything other than a highly subjective view. Instead of res-
urrecting an outdated criterion of 'authority' for the medium, it
makes more sense to see such programmes as one strand in a broader
public debate. Niall Ferguson's *Empire* series for Channel 4 was far
removed from any notion of textbook 'balance'. It was opinion-
ated and insensitive towards less triumphalist perspectives on British
colonialism. But it occasioned an immediate flurry of discussion in
the press. As a step towards a national debate about the legacy of
Britain's imperial past, the series can be rated a success.[33]

History programmes on television tackle big subjects and present
aspects of the past which are, in most cases, rightly considered
to be culturally significant. But they are much less concerned to
prompt reflection about the bearing of the past on the present. This
is why news programmes and documentaries are of such critical
importance. When they offer historical material, topical relevance
is clearly its rationale. As media historian Jean Seaton puts it, real
insight into unfolding stories can be achieved 'only by using reflect-
ive knowledge that is historical in form'.[34] The problem is that the
time-depth of such history is generally very shallow. Within television, history and current affairs exist in almost separate worlds.[35]
In news broadcasting the emphasis on the immediate events of the
day is such that even the most basic historical background tends to
be left out of account. In many instances that reflects the ignorance
of the on-the-spot reporter, dispatched to a flash-point with little or
no historical briefing.[36] But it also reflects an established editorial
judgement about what makes a good news programme. This point
has been effectively demonstrated in the case of the Israel–Palestine
conflict. Understanding this conflict depends on a knowledge of the
perspectives which mould the actions of both parties, and those perspectives are formed by their different experiences of the past. Greg
Philo and his colleagues at the Glasgow Media Group find that not
only is the conflict habitually reported from an Israeli angle, but the
historical antecedents of the Palestinian resistance are consistently

ignored in news bulletins. Thus, out of a large sample of British students interviewed in 2001, only 4 per cent were found to know about the Israelis' forced removal of the Palestinians in 1948. Yet this is the critical base-line of the conflict. Philo documents a consistent bias in favour of Israel on the part of news reporters. But he is well aware that public ignorance about the nature of the conflict is also sustained by the pressure on TV journalists to report action rather than offer explanation.[37]

In many ways, the most effective means of promoting a critically historical perspective on current affairs is through studio discussion. 'Talking heads' can succinctly expose competing perspectives; they can be laid on at short notice to make an up-to-the-minute response; and they are relatively inexpensive. But programmes of news comment have to compete in the schedules with more popular kinds of output. Historians are thinly represented among the range of other constituencies who demand a voice on such programmes. The daily *Newsnight* began transmission in 1989 with the intention of providing a depth of commentary on the news stories of the day. In keeping with that brief, a 'resident historian' was recently appointed, but on *Newsnight* historical perspective for the most part continues to be displaced by other more topical angles on the news. News broadcasting is a critical arena for public history, and one where it needs a great deal more exposure.

No discussion of the arenas in which critical history can be disseminated can be complete without reference to the Internet. It is a distinctly double-edged asset. On the one hand, it is a cost-free means of accessing the world's resources of information, including thousands of historical sites. On the other hand, it is a completely unregulated free market, in which it is often hard to distinguish between the wheat and the chaff. Alongside the scrupulous presentation of primary documentation, there are the historical travesties of cranks, obsessives and extremists. But the History & Policy website, discussed in the previous chapter, is a reminder of the potential of the Internet as a means of following through an agenda of public history. In the six months ending in March 2007, total page views per month averaged almost 15,000.[38]

The clear implication of these varied media is that historians have to make compromises when going public. They may have to submit to the production requirements of commissioning editors. The need to get the message promptly across also alters the conventions of historical writing. Even the History & Policy website, which is under secure academic control, imposes a limit of 4000 words on contributors, on the grounds that only brief position papers are likely to attract the attention of citizens or policy-makers. Scholars contributing to the website are therefore drawn to make more clear-cut statements than they would do in an academic publication. How seriously we view such compromises depends on how much importance we attach to the project of public history. Academic discourse is for academics and students, not the general public. The test for all the exponents of public history is whether they promote public understanding of significant topical issues. In that cause, some of what academics value highly may have to be sacrificed. Historical analysis designed for the public is almost bound to simplify, by removing the stages of argument by which the writer has come to the stated conclusion. This is true of virtually all the contributions to the History & Policy website. The historian has to be taken on trust – until an alternative interpretation is contributed to the public realm. Judging the right balance between directness and scholarly precision is never going to be straightforward. For many academics it is a choice which should not even be attempted. But the potential gains in public understanding are too great to be lightly abandoned. A degree of compromise is surely an appropriate response. And the quality of what has been addressed to the public, both by individual historians and by History & Policy, suggests that workable compromises can be found.

History as democratic discourse

The diversity and unevenness of the history which is publicly available raises the more profound issue of academic authority. For some, it invalidates the whole project of a historically aware citizenry. Critics of history on TV sometimes complain about the arbitrariness with which certain perspectives are foregrounded at the expense of others. Conversely, historians with access to the media may introduce distortions of their own, which are then magnified by the production process. If contradictory readings of the past are so readily available, and so hard to evaluate, how can history be a valid resource? How can history be said to inform public debate if it can be invoked so indiscriminately?

The first point to make is that this sceptical view rests on an exaggerated notion of the relativity of historical knowledge. All historical interpretation proceeds by selection – of themes, sources and frameworks of explanation. But the principle of selection is seldom entirely arbitrary. Chapter 3 described historical perspective in terms of tracing a story back to its antecedents. That too may elicit different narratives. But we should not underestimate the many instances where the main reference points in the story are common ground. The war in Iraq is a case in point. The professional historian will quite rightly insist that Britain did have an earlier history in Iraq, that oil was a growing preoccupation during the period of the Mandate, and that King Faisal owed his survival on the throne to the support of the British. Those facts are not beyond the possibility of challenge, but in the light of current knowledge they are incontrovertible.[39] Even this level of historical knowledge would have been an asset to public understanding in 2003. It would have provided a foundation on which the competing views about the war could have been assessed. Equally, the political debate about the merits of Foundation Hospitals is not likely to be settled by the citing of historical antecedents, but the debate would be on firmer ground if the basic facts were known about the voluntarist system in the 1930s and the tradition of decentralisation within the NHS itself.[40]

However, the kernel of accepted fact is seldom enough to provide an orientation on the present. Beyond it lies the diversity of historical interpretation which surrounds almost any historical theme worth studying. In determining whether conflicting voices are a help or a hindrance to public understanding, much depends on expectations. If the public looks to historians for cut-and-dried analyses and confident predictions, the answer must be negative. 'History speaking' – scholars making pronouncements *ex cathedra* – is a fantasy. Not even Roy Porter believed historians could do that, though in giving guidance about the public policy towards AIDS he played up to the fantasy in order to achieve the maximum impact in an emergency.[41] The furthest that historians can go in achieving finality is by branding some interpretations as *ultra vires*. In the case of the Holocaust, careful scrutiny of the research methods of the leading Holocaust denier served precisely this purpose. David Irving's humiliation in a British court in 2000 did not place the Holocaust beyond controversy: questions continue to be posed about the Nazi rationale for genocide, about the complicity of ordinary Germans, and about the actions of the inmates of the camps. But denial of the Holocaust itself was proven to fly in the face of the evidence.[42]

In the last resort, however, the appeal to history for authority and certainty is misplaced. It overlooks the principal public function of historical debate, which is to keep open an awareness of alternatives. In this sense, even quite acrimonious disputes are a positive asset to public understanding. All too often, the appeal of a politician's prescription is enhanced by the belief that there is no other solution: Margaret Thatcher's TINA – 'there is no alternative' – became a defining feature of her claim to provide strong government. The more open popular knowledge is to the plurality of historical interpretation, the less likely are people to be persuaded by assertions of this kind. What matters is the sense that these issues are open to informed debate, instead of crude stereotyping. This approach is in accordance with the most influential academic approach to citizenship today: the theory of 'deliberative democracy'. According to this theory, democracy is about more than counting heads, and it is more than a mechanism for reconciling interest-groups or legitimising the elite. The essential characteristic of democracy is persuasion by argument. Public issues should be subject to public argument, and that requires a level of knowledge of the facts of the case and the grounds on which those facts can be variously interpreted. Popular debate, in short, is the life-blood of a democratic political culture.[43] This is the context in which the relationship between history and citizenship is strongest. The case has been cogently put by the American historians Joyce Appleby, Lynn Hunt and Margaret Jacob, in their book *Telling the Truth About History* (1997). Reacting to the charge that multicultural history opens the door to relativism, they retort that the true civic function of history is not national consensus but critical enquiry. The clash of historical perspectives not only promotes knowledge of the past, but also opens up a more critical awareness of the present. That is why, in their view, historical debate offers a route to a 'revitalised public'.[44] This is an argument about more than tolerance – important though that is. To have even a limited awareness of the extent of historical debate is to realise something of the range of available alternatives – alternative ways of understanding and alternative solutions.

* * * * * * * *

Talk of promoting citizenship – by historical or other means – can have an uncomfortably elitist ring. When Britain took its first steps towards popular representative democracy, citizenship was indeed instilled from the top. It was equated with an unquestioning patriotism, and it certainly did not promote awareness of alternatives. Citizenship today rests on a much broader definition of political participation. The ideal citizen is more than a member of a community (national or other), more even than someone informed about other communities. He or she has a critical grasp of the contemporary world, able to ask telling questions and able to recognise the limitations of the answers given. History has a major contribution to make towards realising that ideal because of its capacity to surprise, to stimulate and to provoke.

Conclusion

History occupies such an assured and longstanding place in our literary and visual culture that it is easy to take it for granted and to ignore its civic significance. *Why History Matters* has argued that historical scholarship has a great deal to offer the democratic culture of British society. Its contribution is best understood in the context of citizenship. On all sides it is conceded that the exercise of citizenship in Britain is a shadow of what it might be. Taking a considered and informed view on matters of public concern is fundamental to the actions expected of the citizen – in the polling booth, in political parties, and in issue-led association with other citizens. To be effective, representative democracy needs to be deliberative, for which a certain level of relevant knowledge and critical acumen is required. This book has sought to demonstrate that an enlarged scope for public history would be a major step towards these goals.

That there exists some kind of link between historical education and citizenship has long been a commonplace, with material consequences for what children study in school. But the link is too often narrowly conceived within a grid of identity politics, with history cast in the role of endorsing political loyalties – to nation, community or ethnic group. This approach seriously underplays the civic importance of history. Its true remit is much wider and more open-ended, committed not to a particular political vision, but to understanding the societies we live in. Without the insights of applied history, we must be content with living on the surface of things, unable to grasp how our world has come to be, or to detect the direction in which it is moving.

The first practical claim of history on our attention is as an inventory of past experience. History offers unparalleled riches in this respect because the past – even the recent past – was different from the present. Far from condemning history to irrelevance, that principle of difference is what explains history's continuing capacity to instruct and to unsettle – by bringing accumulated experience to bear on current problems, and by reminding us of missed opportunities and paths not taken. History gives us the salutary experience of being startled by the peculiarity of our own age. Sometimes its impact is inspirational, as with the Victorians' preoccupation with the Middle Ages. Sometimes it is technical, as in the case of the many precedents that exist for different emphases in our welfare policies. The tension between the familiar and the strange with which history constantly confronts us is what helps us to find our feet in the world of today, by indicating what is enduring, as against what is new and possibly transient. This central precept informs the way historians deal with historical analogy. Much favoured by the media as a means of closing down debate, analogies are more useful as a means of highlighting the *divergence* between situations which share some features in common; in this way, the distinctiveness of the present is more accurately understood. In the words of Mark Mazower, one of the most thoughtful writers on twentieth-century European history, 'understanding where we stand today ... requires not only seeing how the present resembles the past, but how it differs from it as well'.[1]

Properly exercised, applied history also holds to the other great principle of historicism: that human institutions are explained by tracking their development over time. We cannot fully understand the features of the present unless we see them in motion, positioned in trajectories which link our world with that of our forebears. Without historical perspective we may fail to notice continuities which persist, even in our world of headlong change. In the case of social and cultural formations which sometimes seem to stand outside the process of change – for example, the nation and the 'traditional' family – historical perspective reveals how different it was 'then' and what factors have brought about change. Perception confined to the observed present is particularly stultifying when applied to foreign societies. Contrasting their present with our own too readily produces an impression of the quaint, the bizarre or the outright savage. Historical research reveals the provenance of these stereotypes. Conversely it also brings to light the collective memories of the society in question, and shows how these condition their political culture and their relations with other societies (including our own).

So far as the health of our democratic culture is concerned, the most important feature of 'thinking with history' is that it resists closure. To approach topical issues historically is to 'step outside the box' and to entertain interpretations beyond the reach of present-bound perspectives. History certainly provides evidential weight for points of view which have currency today, but it also brings unfamiliar or forgotten angles of interpretation back into public discourse, as my extended case-study of the Victorian family showed. This openness to diversity of interpretation is what should characterise an independent-minded citizenry. It induces a healthy scepticism about the claims to inevitability or omniscience which are a recurrent feature of our political culture.

These are some of the reasons why the historical profession can potentially provide an important public service. Historians have two tasks: to disseminate those of their findings which bear upon issues of the day, and to promote the widest possible grasp of the merits of 'thinking with history'. Public history in this sense is not just an option to be pursued by a handful of publicity-seeking academics. It is a social obligation. That its record is patchy at best is due to a combination of circumstances: the founding conventions of the profession itself, the way in which applied history has been shockingly abused in the past, and the pressures on academics to write exclusively for their peers. Opportunities to promote the public role of history have been missed. When, during the 1980s, governments in Britain began to demand that university history should re-invent itself as a vocational subject, historians took this to mean an emphasis on generic skills like communication and analysis, which would dilute the historical content of their teaching. What they neglected to do was to take issue with the terms of the official discourse by demonstrating the vocational nature of history itself. Historical awareness and historical perspective are 'transferable' skills, but this point has been lost in the debates about higher education, because few historians see their insights as transferable, and fewer still encourage their students to think in this way.

This is the missing dimension of public history. Many historians have signed up to roles in museums and other heritage institutions, and the idea of a democratic partnership between academics and amateur groups is still very much alive. But the injection of historical perspective into crucial public issues is spasmodic, and few historians see it as an important aspect of their professional work. Of course, a great many themes and topics in history lack any contemporary resonance, and are very unlikely to develop it in the future. But where historical research does touch on agendas of topical debate, it is overly fastidious to withhold the findings from the public on the grounds of academic propriety. The History & Policy website has been foregrounded here, not only because of its careful focus on disseminating applied work, but because it could provide a model for the future. The model is not that of the public intellectual pronouncing on any and every issue of the day, but of academics sharing with the public their own scholarly expertise.[2]

As this book goes to press, Britain's newly appointed Prime Minister is the first to hold a PhD in history. One would like to think that this qualification will inform government policy and its mode of presentation to the public. The record of the past ten years – for much of which there were two history PhDs in the cabinet[3] – does not inspire confidence in this regard, since history was largely airbrushed from the discourse of government and opposition. The prospects for a historically-minded citizenry lie elsewhere: with a reformed school curriculum, with a re-ordered scale of priorities in the media, and with a keener sense of the public interest among academics. The prize is a critically armed and better informed public, providing the basis for a revitalised democratic culture.

Notes

Prologue: Britain in Iraq

1. F. J. Moberly, *The Campaign in Mesopotamia, 1914–1918*, vol. 1 (London, 1923).
2. Marian Kent, *Oil and Empire: British Policy and Mesopotamian Oil, 1900–1920* (London, 1976), p. 157.
3. L. S. Amery, quoted in Peter Sluglett, *Britain in Iraq, 1914–1932* (London, 1976), p. 270.
4. Sluglett, *Britain in Iraq*. See also Charles Tripp, *A History of Iraq* (Cambridge, 2000) and Toby Dodge, *Inventing Iraq: The Failure of Nation Building and a History Denied* (London, 2003).
5. See, for example, 'Blast from the Past', *Guardian*, 19 February 2003.

1 Contending Histories

1. Tony Blair, speech to US Congress, 18 July 2003, www.guardian.co.uk/guardianpolitics/story/0,3605,1000562,00.html-62K
2. Christopher Andrew, Foreword to A. G. Hopkins (ed.), *Globalization in World History* (London, 2002), p. vii.
3. Carl E. Schorske, *Thinking with History: Explorations in the Passage to Modernism* (Princeton, NJ, 1998), p. 3.
4. G. R. Elton, *Return to Essentials* (Cambridge, 1991), p. 8; Peter Mandler, *History and National Life* (London, 2002), p. 146.
5. Philippe Ariès, *Centuries of Childhood* (Harmondsworth, 1973), p. 1.
6. R. H. Tawney, *History and Society* (London, 1978), p. 55.
7. Eric Hobsbawm, *The Age of Extremes: The Short Twentieth Century, 1914–91* (London, 1994), p. 3.

8. Raphael Samuel, 'Back to the Future for the Left', *Guardian*, 18 April 1992.

9. Raphael Samuel, *Island Stories: Unravelling Britain* (London, 1994), p. 205.

10. The classic critiques are Patrick Wright, *On Living in an Old Country* (London, 1985), and Robert Hewison, *The Heritage Industry: Britain in a Climate of Decline* (London, 1987).

11. Prince of Wales, talk delivered for BBC TV's *Restoration* series, September 2003.

12. David Lowenthal, *The Heritage Crusade and the Spoils of History* (London, 1997), p. x.

13. Roy Rosenzweig and David Thelen, *The Presence of the Past: Popular Uses of History in American Life* (New York, 1998).

14. See below, Chapter 5.

15. I am indebted here to the unpublished work of Simon Titley-Bayes: 'Family History in England, c. 1945–2006: Culture, Identity and (im) Mortality', DPhil. thesis, University of York, 2006.

16. Ibid.

17. Eamonn Callan, *Creating Citizens: Political Education and Liberal Democracy* (Oxford, 1997), pp. 101, 107.

18. Denise Riley, *Am I That Name? Feminism and the Category of 'Women' in History* (Basingstoke, 1988), pp. 1–2.

19. Stuart Hall, 'Cultural Identity and Diaspora', in Jonathan Rutherford (ed.), *Identity* (London, 1990), p. 225. See also Paul Gilroy, *The Black Atlantic: Modernity and Double Consciousness* (London, 1993).

20. Pierre Nora, 'Between Memory and History: *les lieux de mémoire*', *Representations* 26 (1989), p. 8.

21. Australia is a case in point. Paula Hamilton, 'Memory Studies and Cultural History', in Hsu-Ming Teo and Richard White (eds), *Cultural History in Australia* (Sydney, 2003), pp. 81–97.

22. Hewison, *Heritage Industry*, p. 136.

23. David Cannadine, 'British History: Past, Present – and Future?', *Past & Present*, 116 (1987), pp. 178, 180.

24. Richard J. Evans, *In Defence of History* (London, 1997).

25. 'Historicism' in this usage is not to be confused with Karl Popper's refiguring of the term to mean 'determinism'. Karl Popper, *The Poverty of Historicism* (London, 1957).

26. Keith Thomas, 'The Life of Learning', *Times Literary Supplement*, 7 December 2001.

27. The classic site for this argument is Michael Oakeshott, *Experience and its Modes* (Cambridge, 1933), pp. 103–5.

28. T. F. Tout, *Collected Papers*, vol. 1 (Manchester, 1932), p. 85 (the paper quoted here was first published in 1920).
29. Richard Cobb, *A Second Identity* (Oxford, 1969), p. 47.
30. V. H. Galbraith, *An Introduction to the Study of History* (London, 1964), p. 59.
31. Mandler, *History and National Life*, p. 10.
32. Keith Jeffrey, lecture given at the XIX International Congress of Historical Sciences, Oslo, 2000.
33. G. R. Elton, *The Practice of History* (London, 1969), p. 66.
34. Roy Porter, in Juliet Gardiner (ed.), *The History Debate* (London, 1990), p. 19.
35. Cobb, *A Second Identity*.
36. Theodore Zeldin, 'Social and Total History', *Journal of Social History*, 10 (1976), p. 245.
37. Mandler, *History and National Life*, pp. 5–6.
38. Ludmilla Jordanova, 'Public History', *History Today*, May 2000, p. 21.
39. Roy Rosenzweig, 'Afterthoughts', in Rosenzweig and Thelen, *Presence of the Past*, p. 188.

2 Other Worlds

1. Christopher Hill, *The World Turned Upside Down* (Harmondsworth, 1975); A. L. Morton, *The World of the Ranters* (London, 1970), p. 71.
2. Hill, *World Turned Upside Down*, p. 14.
3. Ibid., p. 384.
4. Ibid., p. 16.
5. For commentaries on Hill's work, see J. C. Davis, *Fear, Myth and History: The Ranters and the Historians* (Cambridge, 1986), and Barry Reay, 'The World Turned Upside Down: a retrospect', in G. Eley and W. Hunt (eds), *Reviving the English Revolution* (London, 1988).
6. Simon Schama, 'Clio at the Multiplex', *New Yorker*, 19 January 1998, p. 40.
7. Lucien Febvre, 'History and Psychology' (1938), reprinted in Peter Burke (ed.), *A New Kind of History* (London, 1973), pp. 7–8.
8. Ibid., p. 41.
9. Christopher Lasch, *The Culture of Narcissism: American Life in an Age of Diminishing Expectations* (London, 1980), p. xviii.
10. Chris A. Williams, 'Britain's Police Forces: Forever Removed from Democratic Control?', History & Policy website, paper 16 (2003), www.historyandpolicy.org.uk

11. Amongst a huge volume of literature, the following are particularly suggestive: Frank Prochaska, *The Voluntary Impulse* (London, 1988); Anne Digby, *British Welfare Policy: Workhouse to Workfare* (London, 1989); Pat Thane, *Foundations of the Welfare State*, 2nd edn (London, 1996).

12. Michael Alexander, *Medievalism: The Middle Ages in Modern England* (New Haven, CT, and London, 2007); Charles Dellheim, *The Face of the Past: The Preservation of the Medieval Inheritance in Victorian England* (Cambridge, 1982).

13. Keith Joseph, Introduction to Samuel Smiles, *Self-Help* (London, 1986; first published 1859), p. 11.

14. T. C. Smout (ed.), *Victorian Values* (Edinburgh, 1992); Eric Sigsworth (ed.), *In Search of Victorian Values* (Manchester, 1988).

15. Peter Fryer, *Staying Power: The History of Black People in Britain* (London, 1988), pp. 44–50, 67–112.

16. Colin Holmes, *A Tolerant Country? Immigrants, Refugees and Minorities in Britain* (London, 1991), p. 110.

17. Panikos Panayi (ed.), *Racial Violence in Britain in the Nineteenth and Twentieth Centuries*, revised edn (Leicester, 1996).

18. On the black population, see Norma Myers, *Reconstructing the Black Past* (London, 1996), pp. 19–35. I have also drawn on the unpublished work of Paul McGilchrist.

19. Keith Joseph, *Guardian*, 21 October 1974, quoted in Geoffrey Pearson, *Hooligan: A History of Respectable Fears* (London, 1983) pp. 4–5.

20. Ibid.; Peter King, 'Moral Panics and Violent Street Crime, 1750–2000: a Comparative Perspective', in Barry Godfrey, Clive Emsley and Graeme Dunstall (eds), *Comparative Histories of Crime* (Cullompton, 2003), pp. 53–71. For empirical accounts of earlier street crime, see Heather Shore, *Artful Dodgers: Youth and Crime in Early 19th-century London* (Woodbridge, 1999), and Stephen Humphries, *Hooligans and Rebels: An Oral History of Working-Class Childhood and Youth, 1889–1939* (Oxford, 1981).

21. Harry Ferguson, 'Cleveland in History: the Abused Child and Child Protection, 1880–1914', in Roger Cooter (ed.), *In the Name of the Child: Health and Welfare, 1880–1940* (London, 1992), p. 147.

22. George K. Behlmer, *Friends of the Family: The English Home and its Guardians, 1850–1940* (Stanford, CA, 1998), p. 106.

23. Quentin Skinner, 'Meaning and Understanding in the History of Ideas', *History and Theory*, 8 (1969), p. 53.

24. Peter Laslett, *Family Life and Illicit Love in Earlier Generations* (Cambridge, 1977), pp. 3, 181.

25. Leonore Davidoff and Catherine Hall, *Family Fortunes: Men and Women of the English Middle Class, 1780–1850* (London, 1987); John Tosh, *A Man's Place: Masculinity and the Middle-Class Home in Victorian England* (New Haven, CT, and London, 1999).

26. John Demos, *Past, Present and Personal: The Family and the Life-Course in American History* (New York, 1986), p. 68.

27. J. P. Parry, *Democracy and Religion: Gladstone and the Liberal Party, 1867–1875* (Cambridge, 1986); Stephen Koss, *Nonconformity in Modern British Politics* (London, 1975).

28. Eric Hobsbawm, *On History* (London, 1998), p. 27.

29. W. H. Burston, 'The Contribution of History to Education in Citizenship', *History*, 33 (1948), p. 240.

30. Virginia Berridge and Philip Strong, 'AIDS and the Relevance of History', *Social History of Medicine*, 4 (1991), pp. 129–38. See also Hugh Stretton, 'The Botany Bay Project: Historians and the Study of Cities', *Historical Studies*, 19 (1981), pp. 438–9.

31. See, for example, C. A. Bayly, *The Birth of the Modern World, 1780–1914* (Oxford, 2004).

32. William D. Rubinstein, *Genocide: A History* (Harlow, 2004). Some useful distinctions are also made in Eric Hobsbawm, *The New Century* (London, 2000), pp. 18–19.

33. See Chapter 3.

3 Becoming Ourselves

1. John F. Kennedy, quoted in George McGovern, 'The Historian as Policy Analyst', *The Public Historian*, 11 (1989), p. 37.

2. Eric Hobsbawm, *The New Century* (London, 2000), p. 7.

3. Michael Bellesiles, *Arming America: The Origins of a National Gun Culture* (New York, 2000). The controversy over Bellesiles' book is documented in Jon Wiener, *Historians in Trouble: Plagiarism, Fraud and Politics in the Ivory Tower* (New York, 2005).

4. Charles Webster, 'The Parable of the Incompetent Steward', *British Journal of Health Care Management*, 8 (2002), pp. 113–14.

5. John Mohan and Martin Gorsky, *Don't Look Back? Voluntary and Charitable Finance of Hospitals in Britain, Past and Present* (London, 2001), pp. 79–84; Martin Gorsky and John Mohan, *Mutualism and Health Care: British Hospital Contributory Schemes in the Twentieth Century* (Manchester, 2006); Frank Prochaska, *Philanthropy and the Hospitals of London: The King's Fund, 1897–1990* (Oxford, 1992).

6. Richard E. Neustadt and Ernest R. May, *Thinking in Time: The Uses of History for Decision-Makers* (New York, 1986), p. 33.

7. Ilan Pappe, 'Historiophobia or the Enslavement of History: the Role of the 1948 Ethnic Cleansing in the Contemporary Israeli-Palestinian Peace Process', in M. P. Friedman and P. Kenney (eds), *Partisan Histories: The Past in Contemporary Politics* (London, 2005); Eugene Rogan and Avi Shlaim (eds), *The War for Palestine: Rewriting the History of 1948* (Cambridge, 2001).

8. Alastair J. Reid, *United We Stand: A History of Britain's Trade Unions* (London, 2004); Alastair J. Reid, 'Trade Unions: a Foundation of Political Pluralism?', *History & Policy*, paper 5 (2002), www.historyandpolicy.org

9. Fred Halliday, *Two Days that Shook the World* (London, 2002).

10. J. W. Burrow, *A Liberal Descent* (Cambridge, 1981); Valerie E. Chancellor, *History for their Masters: Opinion in the English History Textbook, 1800–1914* (Bath, 1970); Stephen Heathorn, *For Home, Country and Race: Constructing Gender, Class and Englishness in the Elementary School, 1880–1914* (Toronto, 2000).

11. Simon Szreter, 'Health and Wealth', *History & Policy*, paper 34 (2005), www.historyandpolicy.org. See also Simon Szreter, *Health and Wealth: Studies in History and Policy* (Rochester, NY, 2005).

12. Niall Ferguson (ed.), *Virtual History* (London, 1997), pp. 86–8, 228–80.

13. Fernand Braudel, *The Mediterranean and the Mediterranean World in the Age of Philip II*, trans. Sian Reynolds (London, 1975), vol. I, p. 16.

14. Fernand Braudel, 'History and the Social Sciences: the *longue durée*', in *On History*, trans. Sarah Matthews (London, 1980), pp. 10, 26.

15. Ibid.

16. The Historical Handbooks series is evaluated below, Chapter 7.

17. Noel Whiteside, *Bad Times: Unemployment in British Social and Political History* (London, 1991).

18. C. Vann Woodward, *The Strange Career of Jim Crow* (New York, 1955).

19. William S. McFeely, Afterword in C. Vann Woodward, *The Strange Career of Jim Crow*, commemorative edn (New York, 2002), p. 221. See also John Hope Franklin, 'The Historian and Public Policy', in Stephen Vaughn, *The Vital Past: Writings on the Uses of History* (Athens, GA, 1985), pp. 353–6.

20. Alan Bullock, 'Has History Ceased to be Relevant?', *The Historian*, 43 (1994), p. 20.

21. Peter Mandler, 'The Responsibility of the Historian', in H. Jones, K. Ostberg and N. Randeraad (eds), *History on Trial* (Manchester, forthcoming).

22. Bullock, 'Has History Ceased to be Relevant?', p. 20.

23. See, for example, Thomas Friedman, *The World is Flat* (New York, 2005).
24. E. J. Hobsbawm, *The Age of Capital* (London, 1977), ch. 3.
25. Martin Daunton, 'Britain and Globalization since 1850, I: Creating a Global Order, 1850–1914', *Transactions of the Royal Historical Society*, 6th series, 16 (2006), pp. 1–38.
26. C. A. Bayly, *The Birth of the Modern World, 1780–1914* (Oxford, 2004).
27. Tony Ballantyne, 'Empire, Knowledge and Culture: from Proto-globalization to Modern Globalization', in A. G. Hopkins (ed.), *Globalization in World History* (London, 2002), p. 117.
28. Hopkins, *Globalization*, pp. 28–9.
29. Kevin H. O'Rourke and Jeffrey G. Williamson, *Globalization and History: The Evolution of a Nineteenth-Century Atlantic Economy* (Cambridge, MA, 1999), p. 185.
30. A welcome exception is Manfred B. Steger, *Globalization: A Very Short Introduction* (Oxford, 2003).
31. Niall Ferguson, 'Globalization in Interdisciplinary Perspective', in M. D. Bordo, A. M. Taylor and J. G. Williamson (eds), *Globalization in Historical Perspective* (Chicago, 2004), pp. 554–62.
32. Ha-Joon Chang, *Kicking Away the Ladder: Development Strategy in Historical Perspective* (London, 2002).
33. O'Rourke and Williamson, *Globalization and History*, p. 287.
34. Paul Kennedy, *The Rise and Fall of the Great Powers: Economic Change and Military Conflict from 1500 to 2000* (London, 1988), p. 513.
35. Arthur M. Schlesinger, *The Bitter Heritage: Vietnam and American Democracy, 1941–1966* (London, 1967), pp. 97, 101.
36. Bullock, 'Has History Ceased to be Relevant?'
37. See above, p. 50.
38. E. H. Carr, *What is History?* (Harmondsworth, 1964), p. 69.

4   Parallels in the Past

1. Keith Thomas, 'The Life of Learning', *Times Literary Supplement*, 7 December 2001.
2. R. W. Fogel and G. R. Elton, *Which Road to the Past? Two Views of the Past* (New Haven, CT, and London, 1983), pp. 95–7.
3. David Hackett Fischer, *Historians' Fallacies: Toward a Logic of Historical Thought* (London, 1971), p. 258.
4. Ibid., p. 243.
5. Robert F. Kennedy, *Thirteen Days: A Memoir of the Cuban Missile Crisis* (New York, 1999), pp. 97–8.

6. Eric Hobsbawm, *The Age of Extremes: The Short Twentieth Century, 1914–1991* (London, 1994), pp. 2–3.

7. David Reynolds, *In Command of History: Churchill Fighting and Writing the Second World War* (London, 2004).

8. George O. Kent, 'Clio the Tyrant: Historical Analogies and the Meaning of History' (1969), reprinted in Stephen Vaughn (ed.), *The Vital Past: Writings on the Uses of History* (Athens, GA, 1983), pp. 302–10.

9. Ernest R. May, *'Lessons' of the Past: The Use and Misuse of History in American Foreign Policy* (New York, 1973), pp. 52, 82–6; Richard E. Neustadt and Ernest R. May, *Thinking in Time: The Uses of History for Decision-Makers* (New York, 1986), pp. 41–8.

10. Harry S. Truman, *Years of Trial and Hope, 1946–53* (London, 1956), p. 1.

11. Lyndon B. Johnson, 'We Will Stand in Vietnam', quoted in Yuen Foong Khong, *Analogies at War: Korea, Munich, Dien Bien Phu and the Vietnam Decision of 1965* (Princeton, NJ, 1992), p. 49. See also May, *'Lessons' of the Past*, pp. 120–1; Neustadt and May, *Thinking in Time*, pp. 83–90.

12. Tony Blair, quoted by Simon Jenkins in the *Guardian*, 26 April 2006. On the other hand Robin Cook, the Foreign Secretary, drew Tony Blair's attention to the parallel with the Suez crisis: Robin Cook, *The Point of Departure* (London, 2003), pp. 203, 224.

13. Cyril Buffet and Beatrice Heuser (eds), *Haunted by History: Myths in International Relations* (Oxford, 1998), editors' conclusion, p. 269.

14. There were many other incongruities. See Arno J. Mayer, 'Vietnam Analogy: Greece, not Munich' (1968), cited in Fischer, *Historians' Fallacies*, p. 248.

15. Buffet and Heuser, *Haunted by History*.

16. May, *'Lessons' of the Past*, pp. 84, 118–21.

17. David Chuter, 'Munich, or the Blood of Others', in Buffet and Heuser, *Haunted by History*, p. 65.

18. John W. Dower, 'Don't Expect Democracy This Time: Japan and Iraq', *History & Policy*, paper 10 (2003), www.historyandpolicy.org

19. Khong, *Analogies at War*, pp. 148–73. Neustadt and May, *Thinking in Time*, pp. 34–48, 273–83, offer guidance as to how analogies should be managed in this way.

20. Simon Szreter, 'A Central Role for Local Government? The Example of Late Victorian Britain', *History & Policy*, paper 1 (2002), www.historyandpolicy.org; Simon Szreter, *Health and Wealth: Studies in History and Policy* (Rochester, NY, 2005), pp. 220–5, 286–90, 396–406. Nineteenth-century municipalism is analysed at greater length in Tristram Hunt, *Building Jerusalem: The Rise and Fall of the Victorian City*

(London, 2004). See also E. P. Hennock, *Fit and Proper Persons: Ideal and Reality in Nineteenth-Century Urban Government* (London, 1973).

21. Szreter, 'A Central Role for Local Government?'
22. Ibid.
23. Tristram Hunt, 'Past Masters', *Guardian*, 2 June 2004.
24. The tight word limit on contributions to the History & Policy website should be noted here.
25. Virginia Berridge, 'Public or Policy Understanding of History?', *Social History of Medicine*, 16 (2003), p. 521.
26. Jerry White, 'From Herbert Morrison to Command and Control: the Decline of Local Democracy', *History & Policy*, paper 18 (2004), www.historyandpolicy.org. This paper was republished under the same title in *History Workshop Journal*, 59 (2005), pp. 73–82. See also Jerry White, *London in the Twentieth Century: A City and its People* (London, 2001).
27. Anthony Clare, *On Men: Masculinity in Crisis* (London, 2001), p. 69.
28. The material in this and the following four paragraphs is adapted from chapter 1 of my book *Manliness and Masculinities in Nineteenth-Century Britain: Essays on Gender, Family and Empire* (Harlow, 2005).
29. David Rubinstein, *Before the Suffragettes: Women's Emancipation in the 1890s* (Brighton, 1986).
30. A. James Hammerton, *Cruelty and Companionship: Conflict in Nineteenth-Century Married Life* (London, 1992), pp. 143–9.
31. John Tosh, *A Man's Place: Masculinity and the Middle-Class Home in Victorian England* (New Haven, CT, and London, 1999), pp. 172–94.
32. Jeffrey Weeks, *Sex, Politics and Society*, 2nd edn (Harlow, 1989), pp. 87, 107; Michael Rosenthal, *The Character Factory: Baden-Powell and the Origins of the Boy Scout Movement* (London, 1984), pp. 133–4, 297–8.
33. Szreter, 'A Central Role for Local Government?'; Hunt, *Building Jerusalem*; White, 'From Herbert Morrison to Command and Control'.

5   The Family 'in Crisis': a Case-Study

1. *Woman's Own*, 31 October 1987, quoted in John Campbell, *Margaret Thatcher*, vol. II: *The Iron Lady* (London, 2003), p. 530.
2. Margaret Thatcher, speech to General Assembly of the Church of Scotland, 21 May 1988, in Robin Harris (ed.), *The Collected Speeches of Margaret Thatcher* (London, 1997), p. 311.
3. IRN interview with Peter Allen, 5 April 1983.

4. Quoted in Leonore Davidoff and Catherine Hall, 'Home Sweet Home', *New Statesman*, 27 May 1983, p. xiv.

5. Ferdinand Mount, *The Subversive Family* (London, 1982); Campbell, *Iron Lady*, p. 179.

6. Jane Lewis, *Women in Britain since 1945* (Oxford, 1992), p. 12.

7. Pamela Abbott and Claire Wallace, *The Family and the New Right* (London, 1992); Shirley Letwin, *The Anatomy of Thatcherism* (London, 1992).

8. Peter Wilmott and Michael Young, *Family and Kinship in East London* (London, 1957).

9. These estimates are derived from the survey made by the statistician Dudley Baxter in 1868. See Harold Perkin, *The Rise of Professional Society* (London, 1989), p. 29.

10. Michael Anderson, 'How Much has the Family Changed?', *New Society*, 27 October 1983, p. 146.

11. Anthony S. Wohl, 'Sex and the Single Room: Incest among the Victorian Working Classes', in A. S. Wohl (ed.), *The Victorian Family* (London, 1978), pp. 197–216.

12. George K. Behlmer, *Child Abuse and Moral Reform in England, 1870–1908* (Stanford, CA, 1982), pp. 175, 181, 239.

13. John Tosh, *A Man's Place: Masculinity and Middle-Class Domesticity in Victorian England* (New Haven, CT, and London, 1999); A. James Hammerton, *Cruelty and Companionship: Conflict in Nineteenth-Century Married Life* (London, 1992); Peter Gay, *The Bourgeois Experience: Victoria to Freud*, vols I and II (New York, 1984, 1986).

14. Michael Anderson, 'The Social Implications of Demographic Change', in F. M. L. Thompson (ed.), *The Cambridge Social History of Britain, 1750– 1950* (Cambridge, 1990), vol. 2, p. 27.

15. Ibid., p. 49.

16. Michael Anderson, 'The Emergence of the Modern Life Cycle in Britain', *Social History*, 10 (1985), pp. 69–87.

17. Hammerton, *Cruelty and Companionship*.

18. Jose Harris, *Private Lives, Public Spirit: Britain, 1870–1914* (London, 1994), p. 94.

19. Leonore Davidoff, *Worlds Between: Historical Perspectives on Gender and Class* (Cambridge, 1995), chapters 1 and 4.

20. Peter Laslett and Richard Wall (eds), *Household and Family in Past Time* (Cambridge, 1972).

21. Lawrence Stone, *The Family, Sex and Marriage in England, 1500–1800* (London, 1977).

22. Behlmer, *Child Abuse and Moral Reform*; Geoffrey Pearson, *Hooligan: A History of Respectable Fears* (London, 1983), pp. 74–6, 255–6.

23. David Thomson, 'The Welfare of the Elderly in the Past: a Family or Community Responsibility?', in Margaret Pelling and Richard M. Smith (eds), *Life, Death and the Elderly* (London, 1991), p. 202.

24. Christopher Lasch, *Haven in a Heartless World: The Family Besieged* (New York, 1977); for a feminist approach, see Diana Gittins, *The Family in Question: Changing Households and Familiar Ideologies*, 2nd edn (London, 1993), and Leonore Davidoff et al., *The Family Story: Blood, Contract and Intimacy, 1830–1960* (Harlow, 1999).

25. Anthony Giddens, *Runaway World: How Globalization is Re-Shaping Our Lives*, 2nd edn (London, 2003), pp. 59–63; Janet Finch and Penny Summerfield, 'Social Reconstruction and the Emergence of Companionate Marriage, 1945–59', in David Clark (ed.), *Marriage, Domestic Life and Social Change* (London, 1991), pp. 7–10.

26. Lewis, *Women in Britain since 1945*, pp. 65–78.

27. Michael Peplar, *Family Matters: A History of Ideas about the Family since 1945* (Harlow, 2002).

28. Hera Cook, *The Long Revolution: English Women, Sex, and Contraception, 1800–1975* (Oxford, 2004), chapters 12–15.

29. Frank Mort, *Dangerous Sexualities: Medico-Moral Politics in England since 1830* (London, 1987), pp. 37–53; Wally Seccombe, *Weathering the Storm: Working-Class Families from the Industrial Revolution to the Fertility Decline* (London, 1993); Anna Davin, 'Imperialism and Motherhood', *History Workshop Journal*, 5 (1978), pp. 9–66; Peplar, *Family Matters*.

30. John R. Gillis, *A World of Their Own Making: Myth, Ritual and the Quest for Family Values* (Cambridge, MA, 1996), p. 240.

6 History Goes Public

1. Ludmilla Jordanova, 'Public History', *History Today*, 50, no. 5 (May 2000), pp. 20–1, and *History in Practice*, 2nd edn (London, 2006), pp. 126–49.

2. Raphael Samuel, *Theatres of Memory* (London, 1994).

3. Leslie H. Fischel, 'Public History and the Academy', in Barbara J. Howe and Emory L. Kemp, *Public History: An Introduction* (Malabar, 1986), p. 12. See also Robert Kelley, 'Public History: its Origins, Nature and Prospects', *The Public Historian*, 1 (1978), pp. 16–28.

4. Ian Tyrrell, *Historians in Public: The Practice of American History, 1890–1970* (Chicago, 2005).

5. The phrase is Peter Beck's. See Peter J. Beck, *Using History, Making British Policy: The Treasury and the Foreign Office, 1950–76* (Basingstoke, 2006), passim.

6. C. K. Webster, *The Congress of Vienna, 1814–15* (London, 1919), pp. iii–iv.

7. Interview with Gill Bennett, formerly Chief Historian, Foreign and Commonwealth Office, January 2006.

8. Virginia Berridge, 'Public or Policy Understanding of History?', *Social History of Medicine*, 16 (2003), pp. 511–23.

9. Zara Steiner, 'The Historian and the Foreign Office', in Christopher Hill and Pamela Beshoff (eds), *Two Worlds of International Relations: Academics, Practitioners and the Trade in Ideas* (London, 1994), p. 45. See also Beck, *Using History*.

10. Frank Eyck, *G. P. Gooch: A Study in History and Politics* (London, 1982), pp. 337–42.

11. Avner Offer, 'Using the Past in Britain: Retrospect and Prospect', *The Public Historian*, 6 (1984), p. 17.

12. J. R. Seeley, *Lectures and Essays* (London, 1870), p. 296.

13. David Cannadine, *G. M. Trevelyan: A Life in History* (London, 1992), p. 19.

14. Ibid., ch. 4.

15. Catherine A. Cline, 'British Historians and the Treaty of Versailles', *Albion*, 20 (1988), pp. 43–58. See also K. M. Wilson (ed.), *Forging the Collective Memory: Government and International Historians through Two World Wars* (Oxford, 1996).

16. R. H. Tawney, *Equality* (London, 1931).

17. A. F. Pollard, quoted in Keith Robbins, '*History*, the Historical Association and the "national past"', *History*, 66 (1981), p. 421.

18. Robbins, '*History*', p. 425.

19. Theodore Zeldin, 'After Braudel', *The Listener*, 5 November 1981, p. 542.

20. Nicholas Harman, *Dunkirk: The Necessary Myth* (London, 1980).

21. Leonore Davidoff and Catherine Hall, *Family Fortunes: Men and Women of the English Middle Class, 1780–1850* (London, 1987).

22. James Walvin, *Victorian Values* (London, 1987).

23. Michael Anderson, 'Property, Know-how, Fertility: What's Love Got to Do with It?', *Guardian*, 10 February 1982.

24. For important comparable work by historians in the USA, see John Demos, *Past, Present and Personal* (New York, 1986), especially ch. 8; Stephanie Coontz, *The Way We Never Were: American Families and the Nostalgia Trap* (New York, 1992).

25. For example, Michael Howard, 'The Past's Threat to the Future', *Times Literary Supplement*, 7 August 1998.

26. Henry Reynolds, *Why Weren't We Told? A Personal Search for the Truth about Our History* (Ringwood, 1999).

27. James Oliver Horton, 'Patriot Acts: Public History in Public Service', *Journal of American History*, 92 (2005), p. 807.

28. David Anderson, *Histories of the Hanged: Britain's Dirty War in Kenya and the End of Empire* (London, 2005); Caroline Elkins, *Britain's Gulag: The Brutal End of Empire in Kenya* (London, 2005).

29. Richard J. Evans, *Lying about Hitler: History, Holocaust and the David Irving Trial* (London, 2001).

30. Paul Bew, 'The Role of the Historical Adviser and the Bloody Sunday Tribunal', *Historical Research*, 78 (2005), pp. 113–27.

31. Carole Fink, 'A New Historian?', *Contemporary European History*, 14 (2005).

32. Noel Malcolm, *Bosnia: A Short History* (London, 1994), p. xix.

33. Eric Hobsbawm, *The History of the Present* (The Creighton Lecture, London, 1993).

34. *The Age of Revolution, The Age of Capital* and *The Age of Empire*; *Industry and Empire: From 1750 to the Present Day.*

35. Eric Hobsbawm, in *The Times Literary Supplement*, 23 June 1989.

36. Mark Mazower, *Europe's Dark Century* (London, 1998), p. xii.

37. Tony Judt, *Postwar* (London, 2005).

38. Mazower, *Europe's Dark Century*, p. 395.

39. Virginia Berridge, *AIDS in the UK: The Making of Policy, 1981–94* (Oxford, 1996), pp. 1, 7.

40. Ibid., p. 4.

41. *New Society*, 12 December 1986; *British Medical Journal*, 20–7 December 1986.

42. Virginia Berridge and Philip Strong, 'AIDS and the Relevance of History', *Social History of Medicine*, 4 (1991), pp. 129–38; Berridge, *AIDS in the UK*.

43. *British Medical Journal*, 20–7 December 1986.

44. Pat Thane, *Old Age in English History: Past Experiences, Present Issues* (Oxford, 2000), pp. 10–13, 15.

45. Auner Offer, 'Using the Past in Britain', and personal communication, September 2005.

46. James Sharpe, *Judicial Punishment in England* (London, 1990), and Anne Digby, *British Welfare Policy: Workhouse to Workfare* (London, 1989), are partial exceptions.

47. Christopher Andrew, 'Intelligence Analysis Needs to Look Backward Before Looking Forward', *History & Policy*, paper 23 (2004), www.historyandpolicy.org. See also, Charles Townshend, *Terrorism: A Very Short Introduction* (Oxford, 2002).

48. Sheldon Watts, 'World Trade and World Disease', *History & Policy*, paper 7 (2002), www.historyandpolicy.org; see also, Sheldon Watts, *Epidemics and History: Disease, Power and Imperialism* (New Haven, CT, and London, 1997).

49. John Bew, 'Ulster Unionism and a Sense of History', *History & Policy*, paper 15 (2003), www.historyandpolicy.org

50. See above, pp. 69–72.

7   The Citizen's Resource

1. Quoted in Derek Heater, *Citizenship: The Civic Ideal in World History, Politics and Education*, 3rd edn (Manchester, 2004), p. 86.

2. Robert Baden Powell, *Scouting for Boys* (London, 1908).

3. B. J. Elliott, 'The League of Nations Union and History Teaching in England: a Study in Benevolent Bias', *History of Education*, 6 (1977), pp. 131–41.

4. Maxine Berg, *A Woman in History: Eileen Power, 1889–1940* (Cambridge, 1996), p. 223.

5. Guy Whitmarsh, 'The Politics of Political Education: an Episode', *Journal of Curriculum Studies*, 6 (1974), pp. 133–42.

6. Advisory Group on Citizenship, *Citizenship and the Teaching of Democracy in Schools* [the Crick Report] (London, 1998).

7. Bernard Crick, Foreword to James Arthur et al., *Citizenship through Secondary History* (London, 2001), p. xix.

8. Citizenship Programme of study, key stages 3 and 4.

9. Sir Keith Ajegbo, quoted in Mike Baker, 'How About some British History?', http://news.bbc.co.uk

10. Arthur, *Citizenship through Secondary History*, p. 161.

11. History Working Group, Interim Report (1989), quoted in Gordon Batho, *The History of Teaching Civics and Citizenship in English Schools* (London, 1990), p. 97.

12. Quoted in Richard Aldrich (ed.), *History in the National Curriculum* (London, 1991), p. 95.

13. Civitas: www.civitas.org.uk/islandstory/free.htm

14. Peter Lee, 'Walking Backwards into Tomorrow: Historical Consciousness and Understanding History' (2006), and Denis Shemilt, 'The Future of the Past: How Adolescents Make Sense of Past, Present and Future' (2006), both at http://k1.ioe.ac.uk/schools/ah/HistoryinEducation

15. Robert Phillips, *History Teaching, Nationhood and the State: A Study in Educational Politics* (London, 1998), pp. 17–19, 33–5.

16. Denis Shemilt, 'The Caliph's Coin: the Currency of Narrative Frame-works in History Teaching', in Peter Stearns, Peter Seixas and Sam Wineburg (eds), *Knowing, Teaching and Learning History: National and International Perspectives* (New York, 2000), pp. 83–101; Peter Lee, 'Historical Literacy: Theory and Research', *International Journal of Historical Learning, Teaching and Research*, 5 (2004), no. 1.

17. Shemilt, 'The Caliph's Coin', p. 84.

18. Raphael Samuel (ed.), *Patriotism: The Making and Unmaking of British National Identity*, 3 vols (London, 1989).

19. Linda Colley, *Britons: Forging the Nation, 1707–1837* (New Haven, CT, and London, 1992).

20. Raphael Samuel, *Island Stories: Unravelling Britain* (London, 1998).

21. See above, Chapter 1.

22. Catherine Hall, 'Histories, Empires and the Post-colonial Moment', in Iain Chambers and Lidia Curti (eds), *The Post-Colonial Question* (London, 1996).

23. James Walvin, *Passage to Britain: Immigration in British History and Politics* (Harmondsworth, 1984), pp. 219, 182. Walvin's most recent publication in this area is *A Short History of Slavery* (London, 2007), timed to coincide with the bicentenary of the British abolition of the slave trade in 1807.

24. E. P. Thompson, *New Society*, 19 October 1979 and 29 November 1979; E. P. Thompson, *Making History: Writings on History and Culture* (New York, 1994), pp. 154, 164–5.

25. Michael Collyer, 'Secret Agents: Anarchists, Islamists and Responses to Politically Active Refugees in London', *Ethnic and Racial Studies*, 28 (2005), pp. 278–303; Henry Porter, 'We're All Suspects Now', *Independent*, 19 October 2006.

26. Roy Rosenzweig and David Thelen, *The Presence of the Past: Popular Uses of History in American Life* (New York, 1998); Paula Hamilton and Paul Ashton, 'At Home with the Past: Initial Findings from the Survey', *Australian Cultural History*, 23 (2003), pp. 5–30.

27. Elizabeth Yates Webb and Conyers Read, quoted in Ian Tyrrell, *Historians in Public* (Chicago, 2005) p. 95.

28. Ibid., pp. 94–104.

29. Personal information from Daniel Snowman.

30. Margery Perham, *The Colonial Reckoning* (London, 1962); Geoffrey Hosking, *The Awakening of the Soviet Union* (London, 1990).

31. www.bbc.co.uk/radio4/thingsweforgottoremember

32. Arthur Marwick, *The New Nature of History* (Basingstoke, 2001), pp. 234–5.

33. The published version of the TV series is Niall Ferguson, *Empire: How Britain Made the Modern World* (London, 2003).

34. Jean Seaton, *Carnage and the Media: The Making and Breaking of News about Violence* (London, 2005), p. 43.

35. David Cannadine (ed.), *History and the Media* (Basingstoke, 2004), p. 4.

36. Kate Adie, 'History and the Media', conference talk, Institute of Historical Research, December 2002; John Simpson, interview, November 2005.

37. Greg Philo and Mike Berry, *Bad News from Israel* (London, 2004), p. 212.

38. Unpublished returns on History & Policy website activity.

39. See above, pp. 1–4.

40. See above, pp. 45–6.

41. See above, pp. 112–14.

42. Richard J. Evans, *Lying about Hitler: History, Holocaust and the David Irving Trial* (New York, 2001).

43. Amy Gutman and Dennis Thompson, *Why Deliberative Democracy?* (Princeton, NJ, 2004); James S. Fishkin and Peter Laslett (eds), *Debating Deliberative Democracy* (Oxford, 2003).

44. Joyce Appleby, Lynn Hunt and Margaret Jacob, *Telling the Truth about History* (New York, 1997), pp. 283, 309.

Conclusion

1. Mark Mazower, *Europe's Dark Century* (London, 1998), p. 395.

2. On historians as public intellectuals, see Stefan Collini, *Absent Minds: Intellectuals in Britain* (Oxford, 2006), pp. 120, 124.

3. Gordon Brown (Chancellor of the Exchequer) and John Reid (a succession of Cabinet posts, latterly Home Secretary).

Select Bibliography

Aldrich, Richard (ed.), *History in the National Curriculum* (London, 1991).

Anderson, Michael, 'How Much has the Family Changed?', *New Society*, 27 October 1983.

Appleby, Joyce, *A Restless Past: History and the American Public* (Langham, MD, 2005).

Appleby, Joyce, Lynn Hunt and Margaret Jacob, *Telling the Truth about History* (New York, 1997).

Arthur, James et al., *Citizenship through Secondary History* (London, 2001).

Batho, Gordon, *The History of Teaching Civics and Citizenship in English Schools* (London, 1990).

Beck, Peter J., *Using History, Making British Policy: The Treasury and the Foreign Office, 1950–76* (Basingstoke, 2006).

Bédarida, François (ed.), *The Social Responsibility of the Historian* (Oxford, 1994).

Berridge, Virginia, 'Public or Policy Understanding of History?', *Social History of Medicine*, 16 (2003).

Berridge, Virginia and Philip Strong, 'AIDS and the Relevance of History', *Social History of Medicine*, 4 (1991).

Black, Jeremy, *Using History* (London, 2005).

Braudel, Fernand, *The Mediterranean and the Mediterranean World in the Age of Philip II*, trans. Sian Reynolds, 2 vols (London, 1975).

Braudel, Fernand, 'History and the Social Sciences: the *longue durée*', in *On History*, trans. Sarah Matthews (London, 1980).

Buffet, Cyril and Beatrice Heuser (eds), *Haunted by History: Myths in International Relations* (Oxford, 1998).

Bullock, Alan, 'Has History Ceased to be Relevant?', *The Historian*, 43 (1994).

Burston, W. H., 'The Contribution of History to Education in Citizenship', *History*, NS 33 (1948).

Callan, Eamonn, *Creating Citizens: Political Education and Liberal Democracy* (Oxford, 1997).

Cannadine, David, 'British History: Past, Present – and Future?', *Past & Present*, 116 (1987).

Cannadine, David, *G. M. Trevelyan: A Life in History* (London, 1992).

Cannadine, David (ed.), *History and the Media* (Basingstoke, 2004).

Carr, E. H., *What is History?* (Harmondsworth, 1964).

Chancellor, Valerie E., *History for Their Masters: Opinion in the English History Textbook, 1800–1914* (Bath, 1970).

Chang, Ha-Joon, *Kicking Away the Ladder: Development Strategy in Historical Perspective* (London, 2002).

Cline, Catherine A., 'British Historians and the Treaty of Versailles', *Albion*, 20 (1988).

Connell-Smith, Gordon and H. A. Lloyd, *The Relevance of History* (London, 1972).

Coontz, Stephanie, *The Way We Never Were: American Families and the Nostalgia Trap* (New York, 1992).

Daunton, Martin, 'Britain and Globalization since 1850, I: Creating a Global Order, 1850–1914', *Transactions of the Royal Historical Society*, 6th series, 16 (2006).

Demos, John, *Past, Present and Personal: The Family and the Life-Course in American History* (New York, 1986).

Digby, Anne, *British Welfare Policy: Workhouse to Workfare* (London, 1989).

Elliott, B. J., 'The League of Nations Union and History Teaching in England: A Study in Benevolent Bias', *History of Education*, 6 (1977).

Elton, G. R., *The Practice of History* (London, 1969).

Elton, G. R., 'The Historian's Social Function', *Transactions of the Royal Historical Society*, 5th series, 27 (1977).

Elton, G. R., *Return to Essentials* (Cambridge, 1991).

Evans, Richard J., *In Defence of History* (London, 1997).

Evans, Richard J., *Lying about Hitler: History, Holocaust and the David Irving Trial* (London, 2001).

Fentress, James and Chris Wickham, *Social Memory* (Oxford, 1992).

Ferguson, Niall (ed.), *Virtual History* (London, 1997).

Ferro, Marc, *The Use and Abuse of History* (London, 1984).

Fink, Carole, 'A New Historian?', *Contemporary European History*, 14 (2005).

Fischer, David Hackett, *Historians' Fallacies: Towards a Logic of Historical Thought* (London, 1971).

Fishkin, James S. and Peter Laslett (eds), *Debating Deliberative Democracy* (Oxford, 2003).

Friedman, M. P. and P. Kenney (eds), *Partisan Histories: The Past in Contemporary Politics* (London, 2005).

Gardiner, Juliet (ed.), *The History Debate* (London, 1990).

Geyl, Pieter, *Use and Abuse of History* (New Haven, CT, 1955).

Gilroy, Paul, *The Black Atlantic: Modernity and Double Consciousness* (London, 1993).

Gutman, Amy and Dennis Thompson, *Why Deliberative Democracy?* (Princeton, NJ, 2004).

Hall, Stuart, 'Cultural Identity and Diaspora', in Jonathan Rutherford (ed.), *Identity* (London, 1990).

Hamilton, Paula, 'Memory Studies and Cultural History', in Hsu-Ming Teo and Richard White (eds), *Cultural History in Australia* (Sydney, 2003).

Hamilton, Paula and Paul Ashton, 'At Home with the Past: Initial Findings from the Survey', *Australian Cultural History*, 23 (2003).

Heater, Derek, *Citizenship: The Civic Ideal in World History, Politics and Education*, 3rd edn (Manchester, 2004).

Heathorn, Stephen, *For Home, Country and Race: Constructing Gender, Class and Englishness in the Elementary School, 1880–1914* (Toronto, 2000).

Hewison, Robert, *The Heritage Industry: Britain in a Climate of Decline* (London, 1987).

Hill, Christopher, *The World Turned Upside Down* (Harmondsworth, 1975).

Hobsbawm, Eric, *The History of the Present* (The Creighton Lecture, London, 1993).

Hobsbawm, Eric, *The Age of Extremes: The Short Twentieth Century, 1914–91* (London, 1994).

Hobsbawm, Eric, *On History* (London, 1998).

Hobsbawm, Eric, *The New Century* (London, 2000).

Hopkins, A. G. (ed.), *Globalization in World History* (Cambridge, 2002).

Howe, Barbara J. and Emory L. Kemp, *Public History: An Introduction* (Malabar, 1986).

Jones, Harriet, K. Ostberg and N. Randeraad (eds), *History on Trial* (Manchester, forthcoming).

Jordanova, Ludmilla, 'Public History', *History Today*, 50, no. 5 (May 2000).

Jordanova, Ludmilla, *History in Practice*, 2nd edn (London, 2006).

Kaye, Harvey J., *The Powers of the Past* (Minneapolis, MA 1991).

Kelley, Robert, 'Public History: Its Origins, Nature and Prospects', *The Public Historian*, 1 (1978).

Kennedy, Paul, *The Rise and Fall of the Great Powers: Economic Change and Military Conflict from 1500 to 2000* (London, 1988).

Khong, Yuen Foong, *Analogies at War: Korea, Munich, Dien Bien Phu and the Vietnam Decision of 1965* (Princeton, NJ 1992).

Lasch, Christopher, *The Culture of Narcissism: American Life in an Age of Diminishing Expectations* (London, 1980).

Laslett, Peter, *Family Life and Illicit Love in Earlier Generations* (Cambridge, 1977).

Lee, Peter, 'Historical Literacy: Theory and Research', *International Journal of Historical Learning, Teaching and Research*, 5 (2004).

Lee, Peter, 'Walking Backwards into Tomorrow: Historical Consciousness and Understanding History' (2006), http://k1.ioe.ac.uk/schools/ah/ HistoryinEducation

Leerssen, Joep and Ann Rigney (eds), *Historians and Social Values* (Amsterdam, 2000).

Lerner, Gerda, *Why History Matters* (New York, 1997).

Lowenthal, David, *The Heritage Crusade and the Spoils of History* (London, 1997).

Mandler, Peter, *History and National Life* (London, 2002).

May, Ernest R., *'Lessons' of the Past: The Use and Misuse of History in American Foreign Policy* (New York, 1973).

Neustadt, Richard E. and Ernest R. May, *Thinking in Time: The Uses of History for Decision-Makers* (New York, 1986).

Nora, Pierre, 'Between Memory and History: *les lieux de mémoire*', *Representations* 26 (1989).

Oakeshott, Michael, *Experience and its Modes* (Cambridge, 1933).

Offer, Avner, 'Using the Past in Britain: Retrospect and Prospect', *The Public Historian*, 6 (1984).

Pearson, Geoffrey, *Hooligan: A History of Respectable Fears* (London, 1983).

Phillips, Robert, *History Teaching, Nationhood and the State: A Study in Educational Politics* (London, 1998).

Philo, Greg and Mike Berry, *Bad News from Israel* (London, 2004).

Reynolds, David, *In Command of History: Churchill Fighting and Writing the Second World War* (London, 2004).

Robbins, Keith, *'History*, the Historical Association and the "national past" ', *History* 66 (1981).

Rosenzweig, Roy and David Thelen, *The Presence of the Past: Popular Uses of History in American Life* (New York, 1998).

Rutherford, Jonathan (ed.), *Identity* (London, 1990).

Samuel, Raphael (ed.), *Patriotism: The Making and Unmaking of British National Identity*, 3 vols (London, 1989).

Samuel, Raphael, *Theatres of Memory* (London, 1994).

Samuel, Raphael, *Island Stories: Unravelling Britain* (London, 1998).

Schlesinger, Arthur M., *The Bitter Heritage: Vietnam and American Democracy, 1941–1966* (London, 1967).

Schorske, Carl E., *Thinking with History: Explorations on the Passage to Modernism* (Princeton, NJ, 1998).

Sharpe, James, *Judicial Punishment in England* (London, 1990).

Shemilt, Denis, 'The Future of the Past: How Adolescents Make Sense of Past, Present and Future' (2006), http://k1.ioe.ac.uk/schools/ah/ HistoryinEducation

Skinner, Quentin, 'Meaning and Understanding in the History of Ideas', *History and Theory*, 8 (1969).

Southgate, Beverley, *Why Bother with History?* (Harlow, 2000).

Stearns, Peter, Peter Seixas and Sam Wineburg (eds), *Knowing, Teaching and Learning History: National and International Perspectives* (New York, 2000).

Szreter, Simon, *Health and Wealth: Studies in History and Policy* (Rochester, NY, 2005).

Tawney, R. H., *History and Society* (London, 1978).

Thane, Pat, *Old Age in English History: Past Experiences, Present Issues* (Oxford, 2000).

Thomas, Keith, 'The Life of Learning', *Times Literary Supplement*, 7 December 2001.

Thompson, E. P., *Making History: Writings on History and Culture* (New York, 1994).

Tyrrell, Ian, *Historians in Public: The Practice of American History, 1890–1970* (Chicago, IL, 2005).

Vaughn, Stephen (ed.), *The Vital Past: Writings on the Uses of History* (Athens, GA, 1985).

White, Jerry, 'From Herbert Morrison to Command and Control: The Decline of Local Democracy', *History Workshop Journal*, 59 (2005).

Whitmarsh, Gary, 'The Politics of Political Education: an Episode', *Journal of Curriculum Studies*, 6 (1974).

Wiener, Jon, *Historians in Trouble: Plagiarism, Fraud and Politics in the Ivory Tower* (New York, 2005).

Wilson, K. M. (ed.), *Forging the Collective Memory: Government and International Historians through Two World Wars* (Oxford, 1996).

Wright, Patrick, *On Living in an Old Country* (London, 1985).

Zeldin, Theodore, 'Social History and Total History', *Journal of Social History*, 10 (1976).

Index